D0772934

THE WORLD'S GREATEST
ENIGMAS
52 MYSTICAL SITES

WHITE STAR PUBLISHERS

WS White Star Publishers® is a registered trademark
property of De Agostini Libri S.p.A.

© 2015 De Agostini Libri S.p.A.
Via G. da Verrazano, 15
28100 Novara, Italy
www.whitestar.it - www.deagostini.it

Translation: John Venerella and Richard Pierce
Editing: Suzanne Smither

ISBN 978-88-544-0936-1
1 2 3 4 5 6 19 8 17 15

Printed in Malta

THE WORLD'S GREATEST
ENIGMAS

52 MYSTICAL SITES

Preface by
Roberto Giacobbo

Text by
Giulio Di Martino

Contents

Preface

Federico Cesi was an important contributor to our knowledge. A boy who in 1603 – at the age of only 17 years – founded together with three friends an institution that would endure for centuries: the Accademia dei Lincei (literally, "the Academy of the Lynx-eyed," also referred to as the Lincean Academy), one of Italy's most prestigious cultural societies. The name was a tribute to the lynx, proverbial for its *piercing gaze*: accordingly, the gazes of its members were to go beyond the boundaries of *traditional* science. The objects of study for the Academy included all natural sciences, which were to be investigated with observations and experiments that were absolutely free, with no constraint related to office or authority. And it is in the same spirit that, for nearly 10 years, Giulio Di Martino has been traveling all over the planet together with me and my team, on the hunt for many of the unresolved mysteries bequeathed to us by science, archaeology, and history. After many years of broadcasting with RAI (Italy's biggest television company), we have produced many documentaries and pursued many amazing investigations: we dived off the coast of Japan to examine the submerged pyramids of Yonaguni; we scrutinized the timeless faces of the Moai on Easter Island; we descended to the depths of the earth and ascended to its most enigmatic peaks.

We traveled on every means of transportation invented. We shared stories and food with men and women of every race and culture. Ever searching for answers, which often were larger than we are. This new journey, which Giulio undertook alone, brings as its accompanying gift the gazes, emotions, and astonishment of all the adventures experienced together. A volume made up of exciting images, but also of amazing stories, realized with curiosity and seriousness, with an intense desire to know, to explore as far as the *boundaries of knowledge.* Moreover, as the great Marcel Proust wrote: "The only real voyage of discovery consists not in seeking new landscapes, but in having new eyes." The eyes of a lynx.

Roberto Giacobbo

Introduction

"To those who never stop searching"

*"The most beautiful thing we can experience is the
mysterious. It is the source of all true art and science.
He to whom the emotion is a stranger, who can no
longer pause to wonder and stand wrapped in awe,
is as good as dead; his eyes are closed."*

Albert Einstein

I learned about Einstein's ideas on the university benches,
in the theoretical physics department. But I could not
imagine that my scientific degree would dissolve in an ocean
larger than that of scientific research, or that I would end up
immersing myself in the endless depths of the hunt for the
great unresolved mysteries of history and archaeology. Ten
years elapsed between travels and documentaries, theories
and hypotheses, encounters and discoveries. Stories through
images and words, attempting ever to shed light on the most
obscure zones of our knowledge; to meet the challenge cast
by the most enigmatic constructions on our planet; to measure oneself with myths, legends, and civilizations remote
from one another in time and space. To decipher a past that

seems at times to recount a story different than the one we know. And after 10 years, this book. A journey within journeys.

A journey of discovery in 52 mysteries. Fifty-two, like the weeks that make up the year, or like the playing cards in a deck: the two different ways, in fact, that you can browse through this work. The first is to follow a "week by week" itinerary, leading along an ideal path, passing from one page to the following, from one mystery to the next, the one "bordering" on the previous.

So you can fantasize about departing on a year-long trip, crossing over the entire planet, following the traces of its greatest mysteries, stage after stage. Or you can "pick a card, any card" from the deck, letting it correspond to one of the 52 stories in this volume, to amaze you, to take you far away.

In recent years, one of the questions I have been most frequently asked is: "What has your most thrilling trip been, your most amazing mystery?" An easy answer is, paraphrasing the Turkish poet Nazim Hikmet, "Our most splendid journey is the one we have not yet taken." But that would be only a part – elegiac – of the truth. The other part is, rather, what pulsates in the memory.

First of all Rapa Nui, Easter Island. A small triangle of land lost in the Pacific Ocean, thousands of kilometers from everything.

And studded with enormous inscrutable stone faces.

Who do they represent? Why do the inhabitants of a place so separate from the rest of the world appear to have been "damned" into reproducing them? There is a precise point on the island, at the intersection between the edges of two craters, looking 300 m (984 ft) straight down over the ocean, where is easy to get overwhelmed by fantasies about ancient and unknown civilizations. And about what idea they could have had about the meaning of our existence.

You get a similar feeling on the tiny Isla del Sol in Lake Titicaca, a mirror of hypnotic, indescribably blue water. On its shores, the images in my head – slowed by the scarcity of oxygen – attempt to return back in time, to when the mysterious builders of Tiahuanaco erected, perhaps, the capital of a vanished empire, on the shores of that enchanted lake. And then even further back, to millions of years ago, when the Andean uplands were, instead of 4000 m (13,123 ft) above sea level, at the bottom of the ocean, as their fossil seashells would appear to suggest.

Time is a concept you feel compelled, also, to consider while at the top of the steps of the marvelous Maya pyramids in the Yucatán: beyond their aesthetic power, their secret tunnels, their hidden treasures, it is, above all, the obsession this people had about time that suggests you shift your gaze, change your focus. Each of their buildings or monuments seems, in fact, to have been built to measure, to relate, to calculate the passage of time and of the stars. Almost as though wanting to control it, to confine it in an eternal circumference it cannot escape: that is how their legendary calendar works. Cyclical, complicated, perfect. And started up again on 21 December, 2012.

But the wildest and most poignant memory is connected with Uluru in the heart of the Australian desert. Which is perhaps just Nature at her purest. And even there, when the whole desert becomes dark with an implacable black, the gigantic sacred monolith continues to shine vividly its impossible red. A few minutes of genuine magic, and then everything disappears. You feel abandoned, lost in the darkness of a boundless solitude. And it's then that you can imagine what questions must have struck our ancient ancestors, those men who allowed us to become what we are today.

And maybe that is what travel is really for: finding new questions, rather than finding new answers. Like the scientists, as Einstein said, when they are confronted with the mystery. A vital and exhilarating thought: we have not yet figured it all out. Everything is not already here. It has not all been conceived already.

Some claim that we are safe as long as we still have a story to tell. I believe we are safe as long as there still exists a story to go looking for. As another Nobel laureate, José Saramago, wrote in his *Journey to Portugal*: "The journey never ends. Only travelers end. And they may be prolonged in memory, in the recalling, in the narrative. When the traveler sat on the sandy beach and said: 'There is nothing more to see,' he knew it was not true." It never is.

Giulio Di Martino

LOCH NESS
United Kingdom

*The most famous and elusive monster
in history seems to inhabit one
of the most beautiful lakes on the planet.*

The Scottish highlands are without a doubt one of the most beautiful regions of Europe: the rugged mountains, the endless views, the yet untouched nature compose ancient and breathtaking scenery. The center's main region is Inverness, just a few kilometers from a freshwater lake that serves as the backdrop for one of the world's best-known legends, that of the Loch Ness monster. The lake, extending 37 km (23 mi), is one of the largest in the area, and it is in its very deep waters that an ancient and mysterious creatures supposedly lives. For about 80 years it has been chased after by thousands of curious visitors, as well as scientists, magnates, and researchers.

It all began on 2 May, 1933, when an article published in the *Inverness Courier* reported the first sighting of a strange animal in the lake. A couple, Mr. and Mrs. MacKay, claimed to have seen two

AD 565 - The Irish monk St. Columba spots a 'water beast' in Loch Ness.

1933 (May 2) - *The Inverness Courier* publishes an article concerning the sighting of a mysterious creature on the part of Mr. and Mrs. MacKay.

1933 (November) - Hugh Gray takes the first photograph of the supposed monster.

1934 - Robert K. Wilson produces the famous fake known as The Surgeon's Photograph.

1951 - A photograph taken by Lachlan Stuart leads to the supposition that there is more than one 'monster'.

1960 - Timothy Dinsdale shoots the first film that shows a creature moving in the lake.

1987 - In Operation Deepscan, boats with sonar units scan the lake and make contact with three unidentifiable objects.

2009 - Jason Cooke identifies a mysterious shape in Loch Ness seen in Google Earth satellite images.

disturbing humps emerging from the waters at Loch Ness. The episode is reminiscent of "the wild sea beast" described by St. Adomnán of Iona, a 7th-century Irish monk, in his work *Vita Columbae* (a hagiography of St. Columba). That creature came right out of the lake in 565 and it was expelled by St. Columba through the use of the cross and the famous phrase, "You shall go no further."

Six months after the 1933 appearance, the first photograph of the presumed Loch Ness monster was published, with the curved profile of the creature moving in front of the wave, raising several splashes of water. This, like all the following photographs and films, would fuel lively debates among experts, heated confrontations lasting up to the present day.

Among all the various shots of the mysterious creature, the one called "the surgeon's photo" became the icon of the legend. Robert Wilson took the photo in April, 1934, winning a place on various front pages of the times. But it was a fake, discovered 60 years later by researchers at the Loch Ness Centre, who tracked down the small model used by Wilson for orchestrating the hoax.

However, the other images remain controversial. The most famous, snapped in 1951 by Lachlan Stuart, is the one depicting three humps as they wind in and out of the surface of the lake. The first film was taken by Malcolm Irvine, showing nearly a minute of the presumed monster swimming below the surface of the lake. Also suggestive is the 1955 photograph taken by Peter MacNab, who immortalized something extremely long sliding along the surface of the Loch Ness waters near Urquhart Castle; owing to the view of the bastion in the frame, it is possible to estimate that the emerged part of the creature was about 20 m (65 ft) long.

In the 1950s, the popularity of the lake monster reached planetary levels. Curious people from all around the world came to Scotland to hunt for the mysterious creature, which was amicably dubbed Nessie.

Another much-discussed film dating from 1960 was produced by a member of the RAF, Timothy Dinsdale; it showed a hump plowing through the water at great speed, leaving an impressive wake behind. The most recent film of Nessie was made in 2007; shot by Gordon Holmes, it shows a gigantic silhouette swimming in the lake. In August, 2009, even the public satellite images on Google Earth immortalized what seems to be an unknown aquatic creature.

There are those who believe the Loch Ness monster is a collective hallucination, others who believe it is a descendant of the ancient dinosaurs, others who believe it is a timeless monster, and still others who believe it is a series of jokes like Wilson's. In any case, the hunting expeditions seeking Nessie have continued for nearly 80 years, with remarkable deployments of increasingly advanced media and technologies. The entire lake has been scanned, monitored using underwater microphones, filled with enormous lures, repeatedly scanned with increasingly refined sonar, patrolled by submarines, and finally observed by satellites and webcams. Sometimes something unexplainable is recorded, while other times nothing out of the ordinary is found. But every time the case is declared closed, a new sighting calls everything back into question again. Like a monster that reappears from its secret lair after hibernation. Like a legend that can never die.

GLAMIS CASTLE
United Kingdom

*A magical place, shrouded in Scottish
mist and suspended amid Shakespeare,
cruel secrets, and mysterious ghosts.*

In Scotland the idea of mystery immediately evokes ancient castles and ghost stories. And among all the legends of Scottish tradition, the prize for the most ghost-infested castle in Scotland goes without a doubt to Glamis Castle, owing to the sinister "Strathmore Curse" that hovers about the place. It all began in 1372 when Robert II of Scotland, the king who would found the House of Stuart, gave the castle to Sir John Lyon. But a spot of blood on the floor right at the entrance to the castle recalls that in 1034, King Malcolm II was brutally split in two here by the stroke of a claymore, the Scottish two-handed sword. No one has ever succeeded in removing the spot, and it may have been this that inspired Oscar Wilde's short story "The Canterville Ghost."

However, Glamis's most famous ghost is that of Earl Beardie. Legend has it that one Sunday, Lord Beardie couldn't find anyone to play cards with (in fact, the Scottish church banned playing cards on the day of the Lord), and after he had maltreated several servants, he shouted that he would have played even "with the devil himself, until Judgment Day." At that moment, a stranger knocked at the castle and

1034 - King Malcom II of Scotland is killed at Glamis Castle.

1453 - Death of Alexander Lindsay, 4th Earl of Crawford, identified as Earl Beardie, the ghost of Glamis Castle.

1528 - John Lyon, 6th Lord of Glamis, dies and his wife Janet Douglas is accused of having poisoned him.

1537 - Lady Janet Douglas of Glamis is burnt at the stake for witchcraft.

1930 - Princess Margaret (d. 2002), the sister of Queen Elizabeth II, is born in Glamis Castle.

asked to play. The two closed themselves in a room, and no one ever heard anything more of Earl Beardie and the mysterious guest. But those living in the castle swear that during certain nights they have heard strange wails and the loud sound of dice. And many are convinced that they have met the spirit of Lord Beardie, tormented by endless gaming.

Glamis Castle is also the setting for William Shakespeare's *Macbeth*, the place where the protagonist, the general, supposedly assassinated King Duncan. But Macbeth is also the world's most feared drama – from the superstitious point of view – by theater companies; they do not even pronounce its name but rather refer to it as "the Scottish play." And performances of it have been marred by various misfortunes: 22 spectators died in riots stemming from the 1849 New York performance; three stage designers and costume designers died in a 1930 production; in 1948, an actress who was playing Lady Macbeth fell, during the sleepwalking scene, from a height of 5 m (about 16.5 ft). The production of the play has had its own package of fatal incidents and failures: sudden illnesses of actors, stages collapsing, stage weaponry causing actual wounds, entire electrical systems catching on fire. As though the prophecies of Shakespeare's fictional witches had cast a sinister shadow beyond the text.

And it was of witchcraft, in fact, that Janet Douglas, Lady Glamis, was accused in 1537. The castle was requisitioned by King James V and Lady Glamis was burned at the stake. The accusations were proved false and the castle was restored to the family, but ever since that time, the ghost, who became known as the Grey Lady, seemed to appear frequently to visitors to the castle. The family chapel annexed to Glamis Castle can host 46 people. But one of the places is always reserved for the Grey Lady, and no one, even today, dares sit in it.

There is also another female presence that many visitors through the centuries – even exceptional witnesses, such as the sister of the Queen Mother of England, who was born right at Glamis – have sworn having encountered along the corridors of Glamis Castle: the White Lady. Her story is unknown, but the different colors assigned to the two ancient ladies reflect the intensity of their presumed apparitions: the grey one is more subdued, sad, impalpable; the white, more vivid, aggressive, and brilliant.

But beyond these possible influences, the history of the inhabitants of Glamis Castle is marked by many dark events. The most terrible are doubtlessly those involving Count Patrick Strathmore, a dissolute and cruel man, during a war between Clan Lindsay and Clan Ogilvy. There came a point when he was asked asylum by the latter. Not being able to refuse them hospitality, he welcomed them, but then he walled them up in a secret room, where they supposedly died of hunger and privation, after having fed upon one another. Supposedly even today you can hear desperate moans coming from inaccessible places in the castle.

There is another disquieting legend regarding the same Patrick: in another room in the castle, he supposedly locked up for life a child that was born with too much hair and with other never-revealed deformities; this child became known as the monster of Glamis, and he, as well, is mentioned in regard to many repeated sightings.

For centuries, guests, patrons, and researchers have been

chasing after the castle's secret rooms. During a famous reception, the guests were asked to hang a towel out of every window they came across. When they met together outside the castle, they noted that in fully seven windows (but in other versions of the tale, the windows number two or 11), no towel was hanging: a clear sign that some secret rooms existed. The castle is open to the public today: it can be visited, and the most courageous can spend the night there. Lovers of mystery can even decide to celebrate their weddings here, in spite of the centuries-old "Strathmore Curse."

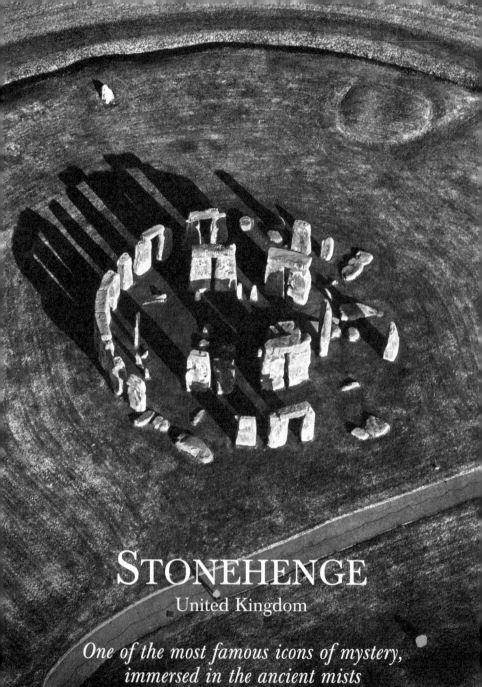

STONEHENGE
United Kingdom

One of the most famous icons of mystery,
immersed in the ancient mists
of the legendary Druids.

One of the greatest enigmas of archaeology is undoubtedly in England, on Salisbury Plain. Stonehenge is a circle of megalithic stones built 5000 years ago. Its name derives from the combination of the words *stone* and *henge* (derived from the Old English *hung*, meaning "hanging" or "suspended"): the suspended stones. Questions about their origin and purpose have forever obsessed scientists and researchers: the treatises, books, studies, and hypotheses on the function of Stonehenge are, quite simply, countless.

The megaliths arranged in a circle display an alignment with the summer solstice, which suggests a link with ancient astronomical knowledge. But there is much more: the prestigious astronomer and mathematician Fred Hoyle hypothesized in 1972 that the entire complex was a refined astronomical calculator. The 56 holes present in the ground would allow precise calculations of the phases of the moon; the ditches would represent the orbits of the sun and moon just as they appeared to the prehistoric men who erected the complex. The astronomic knowledge assumed by Hoyle's hypothesis would be unthinkable for a civilization living 5000 years ago.

But Stonehenge's strength lies in its magical dimension: it was here that the ancient Celtic Druids officiated at their sacred rituals, and it is here, even today, that the

1150 - In his *Vita Merlini*, Geoffrey of Monmouth attributes the construction of Stonehenge to Merlin the Magician.

1740 - The architect John Wood draws up the first accurate map of the monument.

1915 - Cecil Chubb purchases Stonehenge for 6,600 pounds sterling and three years later donates the monument to the United Kingdom.

2008 - Carbon 14 analyses date Stonehenge to the period from 2400 to 2200 BC.

priests of Wicca and other neo-pagan cults celebrate their occult ceremonies. Moreover, the figures of King Arthur and the legendary wizard Merlin are also linked with Stonehenge.

An ancient manuscript still conserved at the library of Corpus Christi College, Cambridge, depicts the circle of stones, embellished by a striking caption: "Stonehenge, near Amesbury in England. In 483 Merlin the Magician bore the Giants' Dance to Stonehenge."

British historian Geoffrey of Monmouth, in his *Vita Merlini* (or *The Life of Merlin*) from 1150, tells how the circular complex – called *Chorea Gigantum*, the Giants' Dance – was transported by means of gigantic beings from Africa as far as Mount Killaraus in Ireland. Then by magic, Merlin transported it over the sea to Salisbury plain: "… Merlin the Magician carried King Uther Pendragon, father of King Arthur, to Stonehenge, and told him: 'this monument shall be the testimony of your victory and that of Emrys. You owe it to the memory of your brother. But realize that it will be said that it is the Giants' Dance and that spirits come to this place, among the stones, every night, awaiting the light that will ignite the morning and give new life to the world.' "

Stonehenge marks a turning point in the construction of megalithic sites. Here, in fact, for the first time, the stones are linked together by a method referred to as the "mortise and tenon" joint: a true revolution for the presumed time of its construction, which highlights the importance and the technological advancement of the construction at the site. The mortise and tenon joint is a solution derived from the world of carpentry: a hole receives a piece specifically shaped to fit it.

But this is not all: the site also is composed of 43 (originally there were probably 80 or 90) so-called *bluestones*, by virtue of the color that they take on in contact with water; these are masses the like of which are not found within a radius of at least 240 km (150 mi), weighing more than a tonne. One wonders how these stones could have been brought to Stonehenge from such a great distance, and why for centuries it was believed that they had miraculous powers.

It probably took centuries to build Stonehenge. Its extremely heavy stones needed to travel hundreds of kilometers and it required a logistic organization involving various generations of ancient Britons. Why all this huge expenditure of energy? Perhaps Stonehenge has yet to reveal its true secret.

A fascinating new hypothesis was formulated in 2003 by Mike Parker Pearson, director of the Stonehenge Riverside Project. Surveys and excavations carried out by the five universities involved in the project have pointed the finger at nearby Durrington Walls, a ring about 20 times as wide as that of Stonehenge that is only 3 km (1.9 mi) away. Inside it is a series of wooden circular monuments and, as at Stonehenge, an avenue that connected it to the River Avon. But while 52 burial places have been found at Stonehenge, none at all have been found at Durrington Walls. All this has led to the suggestion that Stonehenge represented the city of the dead and of ancestors, while Durrington Walls represented that of the living. Stone would represent a hardening through eternity, and wood, the deterioration and impermanence of life. The connection between the two sites is strengthened by the presence of roads connecting them to the River Avon: 3 km (1.9 mi) of road flanked by ditches and embankments. A ritual and metaphoric procession, realized by men of genius from ancient times whose thoughts we are not yet able to decipher.

THE MYSTERIES
OF GLASTONBURY

United Kingdom

Is the legendary island of Avalon here?
Is this the place about which the entire
King Arthur legend turns?

Avalon is the island sung about in many legends, the dwelling of Merlin the Magician, of Morgan le Fay, and of Vivian, the Lady of the Lake. It is the place where the legendary King Arthur was supposedly buried, where the Holy Grail itself might possibly be hidden. A mythical place, one that fog conceals from the eyes of all, except that there is evidence that suggests a different and incredible story.

For thousands of years, the island of Avalon was supposedly circular, surrounded by a shallow inland sea. Covered by a forest of oaks and elms, with a few patches of wild apple trees, it was formed of four hills, one of which, the *Tor*, towered over the others. Two springs issued forth from the foot of this hill; with its 158 m (518 ft) height, the hill was the only thing visible when the fog came up.

With the passing of time, the island disappeared from history and vanished into its perennial mists, entering into legend.

And yet there are some people who believe that at Glastonbury it is possible to find traces of the existence of an actual Avalon. All the elements of the descriptions appear, somehow, to be present. Glastonbury is a small

712 - The Saxon king Ine lays the foundation stone of Glastonbury Abbey.

1184 - The abbey is destroyed by fire and the Benedictine monks rebuild it in Gothic style.

1191 - The abbey monks claim they have found the tomb of King Arthur near the Lady Chapel.

18th century - Robert de Boron writes the poem *Joseph of Arimathea*, in which Glastonbury is associated with Avalon and the Holy Grail.

1539 - The Glastonbury Abbey is closed and abandoned.

city in Somerset in southwestern England. One of its hills has been considered to be magic ever since ancient times, and the inhabitants call it the *Tor*. Centuries ago, seven enormous concentric terraces were carved into its sides, as well as a series of gates opening onto empty fenced areas, on up to the tower of St. Michael's Church rising at the top. The meaning of this complex remains unclear. Other controversial elements are the sources of Glastonbury, only 50 m (164 ft) distant from each other: the White Spring and the Blood Spring. The names are connected with the water issuing forth, milky white from the one, reddish from the other.

Moreover, the zone was rich with yew trees, rendering the place highly suggestive. According to tradition, an apple tree grows upon every enchanted island, and the name Avalon could mean "apple orchard": in Welsh, the word for apple is *aballon*. But in addition to the yew and apple trees at Glastonbury are two other venerated trees: ancient oaks named Gog and Magog, which have forever been considered the traditional point of access to Glastonbury. The sun's rays at dawn on the summer solstice transit the imaginary line joining the Tor with the two trees, as do the sun's rays at sunset on the winter solstice, confirming the importance of these trees. In the 18th century, they were part of a long avenue of oaks made by the Druids.

Chalice Hill is another of Glastonbury's hills, and another point of reference in the alignment of solstices. As its name would indicate, the hill is connected with the legend of the Holy Grail, supposedly hidden there by Joseph of Arimathea. It is said that when he thrust his staff into English soil, the Glastonbury Thorn sprang forth. It still flowers today at Christmas and Easter, and actually belongs to a species originating in the Holy Land. The last abbot of Glastonbury, Michael Whiting, before being killed by Cromwell's men in 1539, supposedly entrusted to his monks a wooden cup described as "the most precious treasure in the abbey," to be concealed in a safe place. Could this possibly be the chalice buried at Chalice Hill?

One fundamental detail keeps Glastonbury from being likened to the legendary Avalon: Glastonbury is not an island. But perhaps it might have been in the past.

The region of Glastonbury is called Somerset, "the summer land," probably because during winter it could not be inhabited as it was submerged. For centuries, the entire area was supposedly an enormous marsh, as also demonstrated by the recent discovery of an ancient village on stilts. Thus, many centuries ago, Glastonbury appeared like an island enveloped by mists, just like the legendary Avalon. English historian Geoffrey of Monmouth narrates in his *Historia Regum Britanniae* that the body of King Arthur was borne to Glastonbury and buried there. In 1190, the presumed tomb of King Arthur was discovered after a Welsh bard revealed the secret of the burial to King Henry II. The tomb was discovered right in Glastonbury, in a pit adjacent to the St. Mary Chapel. The monks even created a false lead cross with the Latin inscription *Hic iacet sepultus inclitus Rex Arturius in insula Avalonia* ("Here lies the famous King Arthur, buried on the island of Avalon."). A false cross that since that time has drawn thousands of pilgrims from all around the world: men and women who visit Glastonbury and imagine it is the mythical Avalon, suspended in the mists of legend.

THE GIANT OF CERNE ABBAS

United Kingdom

*A mystery carved in the chalk,
as large as an entire English hillside.*

The county of Dorset in southern England, with its rolling hills and spellbinding cliffs adorned with nostalgic, solitary lighthouses, has inspired dreamers, writers, and creative people for generations. Its Jurassic Coast is also a unique heritage for geologists, with its 95 km (60 mi) of coastline in which fossils from every age are embedded, telling – like a monumental stone book – of the last 180 million years of our planet.

And right on one of the hills of Dorset, that of Cerne Abbas, a very ancient rebus appears engraved, remaining to be deciphered. It is known as "the giant of Cerne Abbas," or also "the rude giant": it is a pictogram in chalk portraying an imposing nude man brandishing an enormous club. Engraved in the belly of the hill, with channels 30 cm (12 in) deep and equally wide, the huge figure reaches 55 m (188 ft) in height and 51 m (167 ft) in width, allowing it to be seen from all the surrounding valleys. The club alone, which the giant bears in his fist, reaches 37 m (121 ft) in length. The impressive engraving stands out in vivid white, owing to the chalk found just beneath the soil on the hill of Cerne Abbas.

The impressive figure embraces within itself many mysteries: who made it, and in what era,

1694 - The first written testimony of the giant is in the Cerne Abbas parish documents.

1764 - *Gentleman's Magazine* publishes the first drawing of the giant of Cerne Abbas.

1920 - Alexander and George Pitt-Rivers donate the plot with the giant's figure to the United Kingdom.

2012 - On the occasion of the London Olympic Games, some members of the local community reproduce the Olympic torch on the giant's club.

and what was it supposed to represent? The main dispute is about the era of its creation. One possible clue comes from another similar hill, that of Uffington, upon which a powerful white horse is engraved, 114 m long and dug more than 1 m (3.3 ft) deep into the soil of the hill. The Uffington White Horse has in fact been dated to the Bronze Age, about 3000 years ago. Could the giant have been its contemporary?

The construction technique would suggest yes, but the problem lies in the historical sources: the oldest existing testimony of the "giant" dates only to 1694, when the parish of Cerne Abbas commissioned a cleaning and new engraving of the colossal chalk figure for three shillings.

A study conducted by a team of archaeologists in 2008 indicated that a part of the ancient engraving was probably lost: in his left arm, the giant probably was holding a mantle or the skin of an animal. This detail has led to the elaboration of various fantastical theories: on the one hand, there are some who see this as confirmation that the pictogram is an ancient representation of a prehistoric hunter; on the other, there are those who see it as the solution to a rebus engraved over two centuries ago. The skin in the left arm could in fact be that of the legendary Nemean Lion, defeated by Hercules in the first of his 12 labors, which would make the Giant of Cerne Abbas a representation of the Greco-Roman mythological hero.

In keeping with this line of interpretation, the pictogram could be a caricature of Oliver Cromwell, the leader of the Republican revolution from the mid-17th century, who was mockingly dubbed "England's Hercules" by his detractors. The commissioner of the figure, then, could have been

Baron Denzel Holles, owner of the land and outspoken enemy of Cromwell.

Whatever its origin, the giant has watched over the local community since it was engraved into the hill at Cerne Abbas; it has become part of the folklore and legends of all of Dorset. The figure was concealed only for a brief period, during the Second World War.

The British did not want to concede such an easily recognizable landmark to the Nazi Luftwaffe pilots.

Today the Giant of Cerne Abbas is worshipped by neopagan sects, and fertility ceremonies for those unable to have children are celebrated around his phallus. Some couples have even challenged cold full moon nights (as well as British laws) to make love right on the grass composing the giant's genitals, hoping for his powerful, ancient, mysterious blessing.

THE GOSECK
CIRCLE
Germany

The oldest solar observatory ever found,
older even than the legendary Stonehenge.

The state of Saxony in eastern Germany is an aristocratic land, rich with castles, libraries, and art galleries. But the greatest of its treasures is not conserved in any collection or museum; instead, it is engraved deep into the countryside and it is considered the most ancient astronomical observatory of Europe. It is known as Goseck Circle, named for the nearby town in the Burgenlandkreis district. But it has also been dubbed the "German Stonehenge" since it opened to the public in 2005.

The complex is a set of concentric trenches dug into the ground to form a circle 75 m (246 ft) in diameter. Inside, two circular palisades open only at the points of three gates precisely arranged for observing the movements of the sun and stars. The structure would appear to date from the Neolithic period: some artifacts found in the area set the clock back to 5000 BC, fully 2000 years before Stonehenge. And yet, according to official archaeology, the prehistoric man of that period did not possess the mathematical or astronomical knowledge to realize Goseck Circle, let alone use it as an observatory. The incredible German structure seems to want to force us to rewrite history, or to formulate science-fiction hypotheses.

Some pilots discov-

1991 - An aerial survey of the Goseck zone, in Saxony, suggests the presence of an ancient circular structure hidden in the land.

1999 - A very ancient metal disk with astronomical indications is found in Nebra, Germany.

2002 - Francois Bertemes and Peter Biehl of the University of Halle-Wittenberg begin archaeological excavations at the Goseck site.

2005 - The Goseck Circle is opened to the public.

ered the Circle in 1991 as they were flying over Saxony. They noted how the grain was growing in accordance with a strange circular geometry. Originally it consisted of four concentric circles, a tumulus, a ditch, and two wooden palisades at human height, open at three series of gates: one facing southeast, one facing southwest, and one facing north.

A person standing at the center of the circle on the day of the winter solstice 7000 years ago would have seen the sun rising and setting through the two gates facing toward the south. There still is no explanation for the gate facing north.

But Goseck is only the oldest and the most important of an incredible series of similar prehistoric sites scattered throughout the area: more than 200 observatories are distributed throughout Germany, Austria, and Croatia. In this very ancient site, however, it was not just the stars in the heavens that were observed. In this sacred complex, mysterious and forgotten ceremonies took place. Archaeological excavations here have unearthed human bones and skeletons of decapitated animals, probably traces of sacrifices in honor of divinities from an unknown past.

The Goseck Circle seems to resolve another mystery of the past: that of the legendary Nebra Sky Disk. In 1999, an incredible circular metal object was discovered at Nebra, Germany, inside some stone tombs: a bronze disk with a diameter of 32 cm (12.6 in) onto which plaques of gold are attached, depicting the sun, moon, and a series of seven stars – which some researchers have identified as the constellation of the Pleiades – as well as 23 additional stars that have not been identified. Also present are three plaques in the form of an arc, two of which describe the movements of the sun.

The third plaque represents a watercraft, which might refer to the ancient legend of the solar bark responsible for the heavenly journey of the sun by night. The artifact is 3600 years old and is considered the world's first map of the stars. The town of Nebra is only 25 km (15.5 mi) from Goseck Circle: the enigmatic disk could represent a synthesis of all the knowledge of the priests who observed and studied the heavens from the center of the complex at Goseck. In light of these considerations, the barbaric image commonly attributed to ancient central-northern Europe, always depicted as backward and a far cry from Greece or Egypt, needs to be totally reviewed. Does history need to be rewritten? The answer to this question appears to be concealed in the 200 astronomical observatories abandoned in the cold lands of central northern Europe.

THE CARNAC STONES

France

An "army" of stone that has been closing its ranks in Brittany for centuries, almost as though guarding a secret, still inviolate.

In Brittany to the northwest of France stands the largest complex of megaliths on the planet. Nearly 3000 gigantic stones embedded in the ground, sometimes in circles, sometimes in alignments. Whoever realized these cyclopean works, and what their purpose may have been, remain unresolved enigmas. They are known as the megaliths of Carnac, taking their name after a small village in the middle of this incredible book of stone. The entire zone doubtlessly has a millennial history, one that has not yet been entirely reconstructed. One of the most ancient stone constructions in Europe, the tumulus of Kercado, is located right here in the midst of these prehistoric masses, and as early as 10,000 BC, ancient fishermen were burying their dead here.

One can encounter mysterious monuments of every shape and size: in addition to these suggestive alignments, one can also find gallery tombs, dolmens, isolated menhirs, circular tumuluses. From the tumulus of Saint-Michel it is possible to embrace with one's gaze the entire expanse of megaliths on the one side and the tumultuous Brittany coast on the other. The alignment of Le Ménec, preceded by a huge cromlech exceeding 100 m (328 ft) in diameter, is impressive with its 11 parallel rows of mono-

1663 - A chapel is built on the Saint-Michel tumulus; it is rebuilt in 1813 and 1926.

1796 - Théophile-Malo de La Tour d'Auvergne-Corret attributes the construction of the megalithic alignments in Carnac to Druid societies.

1860 - James Miln and Zacharie Le Rouzic begin the first archaeological digs in the area.

1887 - Henri de Cleuziou sees a connection between the alignment of the Carnac megaliths and the solstices.

liths; then, to close the alignment, there is another cromlech of 90 m (295 ft). Not far away are 10 more rows, formed by monoliths varying from 6.5 m (21.3 ft) at the beginning to 60 cm (2.0 ft) at the end: it is the Kermario alignment, translating as "village of the dead." Lost among the various menhir compositions, the colossal "Manio Giant" stands out, an imposing menhir of nearly 6 m (19.7 ft). The third large alignment, then, is that of the Kerlescan, or the "place of cremation," pointing to the east and consisting of 13 parallel rows of 555 stones. The impressive total is about 3000 menhirs, arranged in platoons of 10 or more lines stretching over a length of more than 3 km (1.9 mi). And many have been lost, destroyed, or stolen over time.

There are many hypotheses regarding the ancient men who built all these monuments, and just as many fantasies of those who view this as a sacred place, magical and rich in spiritual energies. According to Professor Alexander Thom, Carnac would be an astronomical clock of colossal proportions, created by prehistoric men to predict seasons and lunar cycles. If this were true, the geometric, algebraic, and astronomic knowledge possessed by these men from the Neolithic era must have been inconceivable. The center of the astronomic complex would have been the Mané-er-Hroek monolith – the "stone of the fairy" – now lying on the ground, struck by lightning in the 18th century. Carved from a single block of granite, and 20 m (65.6 ft) or more in height, it would have been visible within a radius of 13 km (8.1 mi). At any point within the area of the Carnac alignments, it would have been possible to use as a visual reference for sighting the movements of the moon or the sun, for example, or for predicting phenomena such as eclipses. But there are some who maintain that the enormous area of land and the thousands of standing monoliths would have constituted an excessively oversized work for such a purpose. Another widely accepted hypothesis is one that views this as a civilization obsessed with the cult of the dead: the original 5000 stones would have been tributes to the dead, rising from a place characterized by a particularly mystical aura, which, according to devotees of neopaganism, would still be perceptible even today. There are even those who believe that it could be an articulate and enormous sacred area, in which the rows would represent access roads to consecrated circles. Inside these, ancient and mysterious ceremonies would have taken place, the memory of which is now lost. To this day, the name of the civilization that might have created this cult center remains unknown, as do the names of the gods they worshipped. Lastly, a colorful local legend has it that the alignments of Carnac are the remains of a contingent of Roman soldiers who were magically transformed into stone by St. Cornelius, a pope who lived in the 3rd century, to save Brittany from invaders.

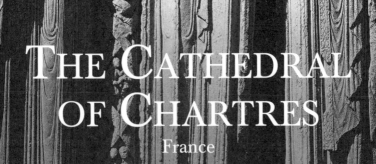

THE CATHEDRAL
OF CHARTRES
France

*A masterpiece of architecture with suggestive
echoes of the Templars and of the legendary
Ark of the Covenant.*

I n 1135, the Cistercian monks began constructing the Cathedral of Our Lady of Chartres (Notre-Dame de Chartres) in the village of Chartres, 95 km (60 mi) southwest of Paris. The religious building presents an architectural plan and intersections that are absolutely unique. The Cistercian order was closely linked to that of the Knights Templar through the figure of Bernard of Clairvaux. And the Knights Templar were the keepers of the knowledge – along with many other secrets – relating to the construction of the cathedrals. Among the Templars' many objectives, however, was also that of gathering and conserving the relics of Christianity, and in this, Chartres may also have played a very important role.

The first phase of work on the Cathedral of Chartres terminated in 1240, 105 years after the start of construction, even though it still lacked the towers and other details. The solemn consecration took place in 1260.

One of the most astonishing elements of Chartres is a labyrinth found on the floor of the cathedral. The number of stones composing it is equal to the number of days of human ges-

1135 - After a fire that strikes the town of Chartres, work is begun on the construction of the new cathedral.

1194 - Another fire obliges the townspeople to rebuild the cathedral, which is the monument we see today.

1260 - The Chartres Cathedral is consecrated in the presence of King Louis IX of France.

1944 - American Army Colonel Welborn Barton Griffith Jr. undertakes a voluntary mission past the enemy lines to verify the presence of German soldiers in the cathedral. Since he sees no enemy troops there, the Allied plan to destroy the great monument is canceled.

tation. For many scholars, this labyrinth would represent an *initiatory journey*: to traverse it from the outside toward the center signifies metaphorically to grow spiritually and be born into a new life. But not only this: the path, which continually varies in distance, becoming closer and farther from the destination, is an allegory of how tortuous the road to enlightenment is and how it puts to the test the true desire to achieve it. The 261 m (856 ft) of pathway inside the labyrinth were to be traveled on the knees, wearing a rosary around the neck and praying ceaselessly. Even today it is possible to witness such a practice performed by spiritual groups on the day of the summer solstice, June 21. The exact same labyrinth can be found at Alatri, not far from Rome, but instead of the large rose motif present at Chartres, a depiction of Christ appears at the center of the Alatri maze.

The mysteries of Chartres are not limited to the labyrinth, but involve all its dimensions: the great central nave, 74 m (243 ft) long, is crossed by an imaginary line, 37 m (121 ft) long, running through the choir. Adding 74 and 37, we obtain 111. This number also appears in many other sites of the Templars; it inextricably links Chartres with Castel del Monte in Puglia and with the pyramid of Cheops in Egypt: all three great monuments, in fact, are located on a straight line that unites them, and in all three the number 111, along with its two elective addends, 74 and 37, recurs in various architectural elements.

Chartres is the only Gothic cathedral that still conserves its original stained-glass windows. They are certainly an artistic masterpiece, a collection unique to the world, with more than 4000 personages represented. Light is one of the great protagonists of the cathedral's magic atmosphere: whether the outside light is dim or bright, the windows seem to glow with the same luminosity. In both daylight and dusk, the windows seem to diffuse the same enchanted aura within the interior of Chartres.

Some think that this effect is due to an external iridescence of the glass, to the secret components with which it was produced. There is also an enigma that no one has yet been able to decipher: in the window of Saint Apollinaire, a small circular space left without stained glass allows a ray of direct light to filter through. This would not be so strange except for the fact that, exactly on the day of the summer solstice, the ray goes to strike the only oblique stone on the floor, in the west end of the nave, one that is whiter than the others, causing to shine a small, golden-colored metal plate inserted especially at that point on the stone. In a cathedral, where nothing is left to chance, and where symbols and metaphors chase after one another, this ancient and sophisticated play of ancient engineering cannot be without significance. No one has yet managed to explain it.

Some have imagined that the great secret of Chartres concerns the legendary Ark of the Covenant: in fact, on a column in the north portal of the Cathedral, there is a representation of the Ark and its sacred contents. And immediately below, an engraving in Medieval Latin reads *Hic Amittitur Archa Federis*, which can be interpreted as "the Ark has been sent here." Perhaps even directly through the order of the Knights Templar. Could it still be buried beneath the splendid and majestic crypt of the mysterious Cathedral of Our Lady of Chartres?

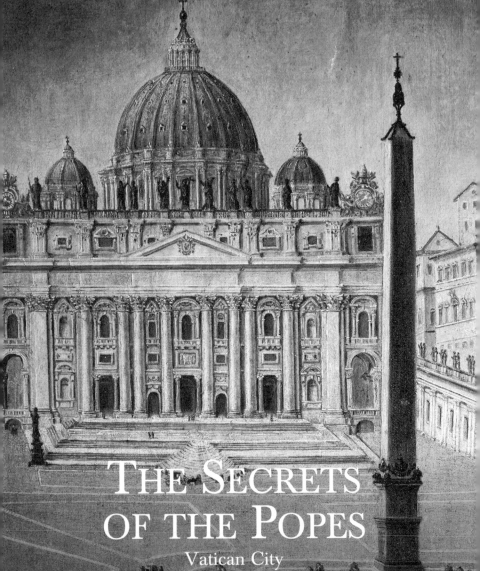

The Secrets
of the Popes

Vatican City

*In the heart of the Eternal City, an ancient secret archive
contains documents that reveal shocking prophecies.*

The Vatican is the heart of Christianity, in Rome, the Eternal City. It is the smallest independent state in the world, but it certainly does lie at the center of history. Its marvelous buildings, the artistic masterpieces that adorn them, the relics contained within them: everything points to the sacred, but also to the power, spiritual and otherwise, that these locations have emanated for centuries. And also to the intrigues and the many secrets hidden in the boundless Vatican libraries.

One of the most incredible pages relating to the Vatican is the prophecy – made by a saint – about the end of the Catholic Church itself: the prophecy of St. Malachy. His most disturbing passage reads: "During the last persecution of the Holy Roman Church, Peter the Roman will sit, and he will shepherd the flocks among many tribulations; once these have passed, the City of Seven Hills will collapse, and the Dreadful Judge will judge his people. Amen."

According to legend, St. Malachy received a vision indicating all the popes who, from that day forward, would rise to the papal throne. This occurred in 1148 but the manuscripts were published only in 1595, as the *Prophetia de summis pontificibus*, drawn up by the Benedictine monk

1143 - Celestine II is elected Pope, the first one mentioned in the prophecy of St. Malachy.

1148 - Death of St. Malachy, archbishop of Armagh, considered the author of the prophecies concerning the popes.

1595 - The Benedictine monk Arnold Wion publishes the Prophecy of St. Malachy for the first time in his *Lignum vitae*.

2013 - Pope Benedict XVI abdicates and the Argentine Jorge Mario Bergoglio is elected Pope, choosing Francis as his papal name.

Arnold Wion. It is a list of 112 popes: to each pope, one line is dedicated, a few words in Latin anticipating his election. The list begins with Celestine II and seems to end right at Benedict XVI. The first pope on the list, Celestine II, is announced with the phrase *Ex castro Tiberis*, which one can translate as "from a castle on the Tiber": the pontiff, indeed, was a native of Città di Castello ("the city of the castle"), the first Umbrian center in the upper valley of the Tiber River.

For Lucius II, the prophecy announces: *Inimicus expulsus*, meaning "the enemy expelled," and the surname of the future pope was nothing other than Caccianemici (literally, "enemy-chaser"). The famous Celestine V was prophesied by the phrase *Ex eremo celsus*, "elevated from the hermitage": Pietro da Morrone was indeed a hermit.

Even if the coincidences seem impressive, we must always remember that there is a broad margin of personal discretion in the retrospective interpretation of a prophecy. The 107th pope predicted by St. Malachy is identified by the phrase *Pastor et Nauta*, "shepherd and mariner." Angelo Roncalli was a man of humble origins (*pastor*) and he was Patriarch of Venice, the city on the water. Number 108 is prophesied as *Flos Florum*, that is, "the flower of flowers." In the coat of arms of Giovanbattista Montini, the future Pope Paul VI, three lilies appear; this plant has always been called "the flower of flowers." In 1978, it was Albino Luciani who rose to the papal throne: his pontificate, however, lasted only 33 days, and for him, St. Malachy had predicted: *De medietate lunae*, which some have interpreted as "the time of one moon," just the duration of his papacy. The next 27 years were those of John Paul II, who is announced in the prophecy as *De Labore Solis*, which can be translated as "by the effort of the sun." Some people have interpreted the prophecy with the consideration that Karol Wojtyla was the pope who visited more countries than any other. Lastly, for the final pope predicted by the sayings of Malachy, we read the phrase *Gloria Olivae*. Many connect the papacy of Pope Benedict XVI with the olive tree, the symbol of peace. Benedict XVI is thus the last pope to whom the prophecy dedicates just one line. Then would come the time of Peter the Roman, and with him, the end of the Catholic Church. Thus, the election of Pope Francis I after the sensational abdication of his predecessor, triggers new interpretations of St. Malachy's prophecy and of the destiny of the Church itself as an institution. Just as Peter received the mandate from Jesus to build his Church, so would Peter II return the Church to Christ. A circle that closes itself perfectly.

That is, assuming you want to believe in the prophecies of the saint.

CASTEL DEL MONTE
Italy

In southern Italy, halfway between France and Egypt, a majestic and incomprehensible edifice challenges hunters of secrets.

Castel del Monte is one of the most enigmatic castles in the world. Built on top of a hill 465 m (about 500 yards) high, it lies on the imaginary line connecting Jerusalem with Rome. In the 13th century, this is how far the Holy Roman Empire extended, governed by Frederick II of Swabia, the ruler known as *Stupor mundi*, "the wonder of the world." It is uncertain when the castle was built – it is assumed to have been built between 1230 and 1240 – just as its intended purpose is unknown. There are no moats or drawbridges for defending against enemy attacks, nor are there spaces for lodging garrisons, stocks, kitchens, or storerooms. Some have advanced the hypothesis that it might have been a hunting lodge, or a stopover place from which the sovereign departed on his hunting trips, but there remains the stumbling block of the excessive majesty of the building. Many agree, however, that Frederick II had built it in keeping with a quite precise, secret design. Nothing here seems to have been left to chance, beginning even with the choice of location. Castel del Monte is located about halfway between the Cathedral of Chartres and the great

1194 - Frederick II is born in Jesi.

1198 - Frederick II is crowned King of Sicily.

1220 - Frederick II is crowned Emperor of the Holy Roman Empire.

1227 - Pope Gregory IX excommunicates Frederick II for not having participated in the Fifth Crusade.

1228 - Frederick II takes part in the Sixth Crusade and is crowned King of Jerusalem.

1240 - Frederick II commissions Riccardo da Montefuscolo to build the Castel del Monte.

1250 - Frederick II dies in Fiorentino di Puglia.

pyramid of Cheops, exactly along the line that unites them. Considering that it is the last of the three monuments to have been built, could this be pure coincidence?

But that is not all: the plan of the castle is octagonal; there are eight towers, each also of octagonal plan. On each of the two floors are eight rooms with windows facing onto an inner courtyard, also octagonal, and at the center of this there was originally a basin, also with eight sides. On the external portal and at the entrances to the various rooms are representations of various types of flowers in groups of eight. There are also petals in groups of eight on the capitals of the rooms, and other details of the construction represent the number eight in an obsessive manner. No explanation has yet been found for the recurrence of this number.

Frederick II of Swabia was attracted by the Orient. Even though he ruled the Holy Roman Empire, he was excommunicated twice and waged war against the papacy. His court, a rare example of magnificence, was frequented by poets, magicians, and alchemists. For the esoteric tradition, the octagon was the figure that united earth and heaven. Historically, in baptisteries, usually of octagonal plan, this form was a tribute to the relationship between the infant and God. There is also another number that recurs and that would seem to link the Castel del Monte with ancient Egypt. The number 111 (calculated in cubits, the unit of measure of the Egyptians) turns out to be one of the key numbers in the great pyramid of Giza, along with its two addends, 74 and 37 (the same numbers often return in the mysterious Cathedral of Chartres). The sum of the widths of the six visible faces of each of the eight towers of Castel del Monte is equal to 37 Egyptian cubits, and the sum of the lengths of the walls of the courtyard is equal to 111 Egyptian cubits. And not only did Frederick II use numbers that were dear to the Egyptians, but he also took inspiration from their method of construction. In fact, on particular days, the shadows projected by the sun indicate quite precise points. And furthermore, 26 December, 1194 is the date of the birth of Frederick II, who lived for 56 years; six façades for each of the eight octagonal towers make 48, which, when added to the eight outer walls, give 56, the exact number of years that the emperor lived.

Simply games with numbers? Perhaps. But there are some who believe that the impressive construction was an enormous safe erected to enclose a legendary object: the Holy Grail. The entire castle would represent the legendary lost chalice. When Frederick II died in 1250, he was robed, as he had asked to be, in the habit of the Cistercian monks, the order that built the Temple of Chartres and inspired the Knights Templar. For some, this would be a further indication that the sacred relic had passed through or is still hidden within the emperor's spectacular castle.

In Dracula's Court

Romania

Amid history and legend, Transylvania is home to several places that were the scenes of Prince Vlad's cruel atrocities.

Created by Irish writer Bram Stoker in 1897, Dracula is one of the symbolic personages of the horror genre. Ever since the day his eponymous novel was published, many researchers have attempted to identify real traces of his story, to identify what actually existing person might have inspired Stoker's vampire, and to determine the location of his sinister castle.

The vampire is one of the oldest figures in mythology. In ancient Babylonia, in Egypt, in South America, nearly all civilizations have tales of undead creatures who chase after living beings. But Stoker chose Romania as the location for his novel. The reason for this choice may be based on its unique combination of elements: wilderness, Gothic cities, and a bloodthirsty prince. Romania is a very mysterious place, perhaps the most enigmatic of Europe. And in this region, Dracula is not only a character in a novel, but his name also refers to a murderer in the flesh, a notorious nobleman who lived in the 15th century, Vlad III Dracula. Nicknamed Vlad Tepes – Vlad the Impaler – he was the son of Vlad Dràcul, an obscure member of the Order of the Dragon, and in those times, the word for dragon translated as

1431 - Vlad III Dracula is born in Transylvania.

1436 - Vlad II Dràcul, Vlad III's father, becomes Prince of Walachia.

1448 - Vlad III becomes Prince of Wallachia.

1462 - Vlad III defeats the army of the Ottoman sultan Muhammad II, but a few months later he himself is defeated and imprisoned.

1476 - Vlad III dies in battle against the Turks.

1897 - Bram Stoker publishes the novel *Dracula*.

"devil." The members of this order wore long black cloaks and red caps.

Vlad was born around 1431 at Sighişoara, which today is one of the best-conserved medieval fortresses of Europe, called the "Pearl of Transylvania." The house where Vlad was born is known today by the name of Casa Dràcul, and it is marked by a sign and the emblem of the Dragon. The medieval fresco inside is the only known portrait of Vlad Dràcul. Just three doors ahead, in the belly of a gigantic bell tower, there is a museum conserving chilling examples of some of Vlad's favorite torture instruments.

The mad exploits of Dracula were already being recounted in the mid-15th century. The protagonist, who actually lived, was a warlord, the prince of Wallachia, a region now in Romania. Already in life he was considered a bloodthirsty monster, and his reputation grew with the passing of time. Crowds filled the streets throughout Europe to hear the latest macabre exploits of Dracula, famous for his perverse pleasure in personally torturing and killing his enemies. There are numerous traits in common between the character of Dracula, created by Bram Stoker, and Vlad III, the primary of which was an obsession for other people's blood.

Wallachia was the kingdom of Vlad Dracula, and perhaps the realm of the true vampire: today Targovişte, the capital and fortress of Vlad Dracula, is in ruins. The most imposing structure still standing is the Tower of Chindia, built by the prince himself. It was probably here that he plotted some of his bloodiest revenge. The prisoners who were spared impalement were sent to build the dark Poenari Castle 80 km (50 mi) away. This was an ancient fortress that Vlad had decided to restore in order to make it his own citadel. Defined as "the citadel of the prince of darkness," this was the real lair of Dracula.

However, Bram Stoker set his novel along Borgo Pass, a very old road in an enchanting mountain region, the area of the lower Carpathians. The rugged mountains looming on the horizon evoke an eerie atmosphere, but in reality, no traces of the castle of Dracula exist.

Stoker's description actually resembles the architecture of Bran Castle, which stands out over the Gothic city of Braşov: appearing by day as an enchanting castle, by night, it looks like a sinister hideout. The narrow stairway and the forest surrounding the manor bring goose bumps to many. Today Bran Castle is one of Romania's national monuments. Rising from the ruins of an ancient fortress of the Teutonic Knights, it was built in 1377. But certain details do not correspond to the refuge of Dracula described by Stoker: for example, there is no great river flowing near the castle. Certainly the tangled forests and Gothic landscapes of Transylvania have fueled the portrait drawn by Stoker of the realm of Dracula. But which is the true Castle of Dracula and where the real tomb of Vlad Tepes can be found remain mysteries.

THE PYRAMIDS OF VISOKO
Bosnia

*A controversial excavation campaign in
Bosnia-Herzegovina suggests that the largest
pyramids of Europe may be hidden beneath
three green hills.*

In the heart of Bosnia-Herzegovina, a few kilometers from the capital, Sarajevo, rise three hills that for years have been provoking fierce debate in the archaeological world. Bosnian-American archaeologist Semir Osmanagich claims that in 2005 he discovered the largest and most ancient pyramids on our planet. According to the archaeologist, the three hills rising around the village of Visoko would in fact be colossal pyramids, covered by centuries-old layers of vegetation. Proceeding with excavation is not easy, not only because of the hostility on the part of the academic world toward Osmanagich's hypothesis, but also because numerous minefields are present in the zone, a sad legacy of the civil war from the 1990s. The entire site has been dubbed "the Valley of the Pyramids," and the emerging archaeological structures have been called the Pyramids of the Sun, of the Moon, and of the Dragon. In order to understand the scope of the alleged discovery, the Pyramid of the Sun, once "liberated" from the hill, would reach 220 m (722 ft) in height, higher than the Great Pyramid of Khufu (Cheops) in Egypt.

Osmanagich says, "This is the largest complex ever built upon our planet. In the valley of Visoko, there are three large four-sided pyramidal structures. The

2005 - The archaeologist Semir Osmanagich claims he has found three huge pyramids near the village of Visoko.

2006 - Osmanagich begins excavating the hills.

2006 - The *Times* publishes a letter written by Anthony Harding, President of the European Association of Archaeologists, who rejects Osmanagich's theories as absurd.

2011 - A Sarajevo court officially grants permission to continue the archaeological research on the Visoko hills after a legal dispute that lasts four years.

construction of the pyramids was realized in accordance with these very principles. We must, however, succeed in demonstrating that these monuments are human artifacts. The blocks of stone recovered from the site are cement, cement of an excellent quality, even better than what we produce today. The fact that it has resisted for several thousands of years demonstrates that it is material of a superior quality."

Satellite imagery has shown how the three hills appear to be hiding some structures of pyramidal inspiration and how they appear to be oriented in accordance with the cardinal axes. But if the monumental complex discovered actually does exist on Bosnian ground, it remains to be revealed who could have produced it and when. In this zone, there are no traces of a civilization capable of constructing such monuments during the period of the presumed dating of the site, that is, 10,000 BC.

Osmanagich also affirms, "As our geological and archaeological research gradually proceeds, we find growing evidence demonstrating the human matrix of these immense monuments. The enormous slabs of sandstone are clearly worked by human hand. I think it would be obvious even to the eyes of a five-year-old child. About 1 m (3.3 ft) deep, under a layer of earth, we have found sandstone slabs arranged in perfect order. Furthermore, when we performed material analysis on it, we discovered that it is an adhesive connective material, the presence of which is also been found in the Pyramids of the Sun and of the Moon. This means that the three Bosnian pyramids were built by the same hand, using one same adhesive material."

Moreover, the points at which the three hills rise form the vertices of an equilateral triangle, which indeed causes one to think of an architectural design of human matrix. And it is not the only coincidence, as Osmanagich explains: "When we began baring the walls and terraces of these monuments, we discovered an interesting rectangular structure on the Pyramid of the Moon. It is singular to note how these two pyramids, together with that of the Dragon, are arranged in such a manner as to form a triangle, each about 2.2 km (1.4 mi) from the others. What is the probability that nature could have produced these three hills, having exactly the same design – four sides, a triangular form, a flat summit, a perfect orientation with the cardinal points – and with the three together forming an equilateral triangle? I would say none. And then, near the top of the pyramid, we find more sandstone. The position of the sandstone slab is vertical and, as we know, nature does not put things vertically."

It is suggestive to visit the excavations at Visoko, to walk on the pavements: the stones unearthed make one dream of and imagine unknown realities. But there are also some who shout "sacrilege!" Garrett Fagan of Pennsylvania State University, declares, "They should not be allowed to destroy genuine sites in the pursuit of these delusions [...] It's as if someone were given permission to bulldoze Stonehenge to find secret chambers of lost ancient wisdom underneath." Fantasy or reality? The upcoming years will tell us whether we have to rewrite the history of archaeology and of the ancient civilizations that have preceded us.

THE ORACLE
OF DELPHI

Greece

In ancient times, sovereigns and commanders
came to this place to know their future;
artists and poets came to receive inspiration.

The Greek site of Delphi, built beginning in the 7th century BC, was considered the *omphalos* or navel of the then-known world: according to myth, Zeus chose it as such because two eagles that he had set in flight from two extreme ends of the earth came to land there at the same time. And the traveler who visits the valley of Delphi today cannot help but notice the presence of the ancient divinities in one of the world's most famous sacred areas, one of the greatest centers of ancient Greece.

Omphalos is also the name of the stone (now conserved in the Museum of Delphi) beside which the priestess of Apollo was able to predict the future. There are many mysteries contained within the numerous variants of the myths connected with the Oracle of Delphi.

In order to understand the origin of the name Delphi, we must refer to the myth. A Homeric hymn tells how the god Apollo transformed himself into a dolphin (*delphìs*, in fact, in Greek), jumped onto a ship sailing from Crete and forced the sailors to land at Crisa, the port closest to the Valley of Delphi, and become his priests. According to other myths, Delphine/Daphne ("the bloody one") was the

8th century BC - During the Mycenaean period there is evidence of the cult of Mother Earth (Gaea) and the dragon-like Python at Delphi.

7th century BC - The original core of the sanctuary of Delphi is constructed.

582 BC - Establishment of the first Pythian Games, which are held every four years and are open to athletes from all parts of Greece.

356 BC - The Phocians occupy the Delphi sanctuary, thus triggering the Third Holy War, which is won a decade later by Philip II of Macedon.

name of the prophetess of Mother Earth (Gaea) from whom Apollo usurped the art of predicting the future, by desecrating her temple, killing her, and taking possession of the art of divination. Plutarch, the Greek historian who was also a priest of the Delphi sanctuary in the times of Roman domination, tells of a mysterious ancient rite that appears to refer to this myth. In his work *The Obsolescence of Oracles*, Plutarch writes: "Every nine years on the threshold of the Temple of Delphi, a hut was built in the style of a royal residence, and a night attack was simulated [...] The table on which they had arranged the first fruits was overturned, the hut was set on fire, and the men bearing torches went away without looking back. Then the young man who had led the assault made his way to Tempe to purify himself, and he returned from there in triumph crowned with laurel and with a branch of laurel in hand..."

According to myth, the first sanctuary was erected with beeswax and feathers; the second was made of ferns; the third, with branches of laurel; the fourth was erected in bronze, by Hephaestus, with birds of gold singing at the top of it; the fifth, of stone, was destroyed by fire and then reconstructed in its definitive form.

It is certain that a female divinity, represented in many statuettes found in the deepest layers of archaeological excavations, was venerated at Delphi since the end of the 14th century BC (fully seven centuries before the construction of the sanctuary). An ancient shrine dedicated to Mother Earth was founded by the Cretans. Hellenic peoples who migrated from the north and arrived at Delphi eventually replaced the cult of Mother Earth with that of Apollo.

At the time of the Greek colonization of the Mediterranean,

each city state consulted the Oracle to know how and where to implement its own campaigns of conquest. At Delphi each city erected its own Thesaurus (literally, "treasure store"), a building for depositing offerings, leading to rivalry in generosity.

The precious ex-votos testified to the devotion of faithful cities and individuals to the oracle. Thus, in a short time, the sanctuary of Apollo became an international observatory that, through its very powerful college of priests, conditioned foreign politics of the time.

The power of the oracle was enormous: it was capable of triggering conflicts and wars. When the Pythia, the prophetess of the god, inhaled fumes from the crevice where the mythological serpent Python was killed, and then chewed laurel leaves (a plant sacred to Apollo), she went into a trance and began issuing prophecies in the abstruse and confused language of the oracle.

Foreigners as well went to consult the oracle of Apollo: Croesus, the king of Lydia, offered precious metals (of such a fabulous weight as to arouse astonishment) when he went to ask the prophetess whether he should fight against the king of Persia. The Pythia prophesied that if he crossed the River Halys, a great empire would fall. Galvanized by this response, Croesus forgot to ask which empire, and embarked upon war: the great empire that fell, however, was his own.

Moreover, every prophecy is, by its very nature, ambiguous. There remains yet the mystery of the intoxicating and divinatory properties of the fumes released from the crevice – mentioned by Diodorus and Plutarch – which were perhaps composed of hydrocarbon gases and are still perceptible.

And perhaps still capable of inspiring new oracles.

ATLANTIS
Greece

*The legendary Lost Continent described
by Plato could have many ties with
the marvelous island of Santorini.*

Atlantis is the myth of myths. Legend has it that a very ancient and incredibly involved civilization inhabited our planet before any other known civilization. And it disappeared in a cataclysm that annihilated the continent, plunging all traces of it forever into the abyss. Moreover, all our knowledge derives from what the inhabitants of Atlantis succeeded in passing down to us.

We owe the name of Atlantis to Plato: the legendary vanished civilization is cited in two famous dialogues of the Greek philosopher. In *Timaeus*, written around 360 BC, we read: "Before that narrow strait known as the Pillars of Hercules, there was an island. And this island was larger than Libya and Asia together, and from that one could pass to other islands, and from these, to the mainland opposite. [...] In later times [...], there were earthquakes and extraordinary cataclysms, so that in the course of one day and a dreadful night [...] everything, as a whole, sank into the earth. And thus swallowed up by the sea, Atlantis vanished." Also in Plato's writings, there is a careful description of the capital of the Lost Continent: "While all around the city there

1456 BC - An eruption of the volcano on the island of Thera has a devastating effect on the civilizations of the eastern Mediterranean.

c. 360 BC - Plato writes the dialogues *Critias* and *Timaeus*, in which he introduces the Atlantis myth.

1627 - The English philosopher Francis Bacon describes a utopian society in his *The New Atlantis*.

1882 - Ignatius Loyola Donnelly publishes *Atlantis: the Antediluvian World*, a book that stirs a great deal of interest in the lost continent among the general public.

was a plain embracing the city, and this in turn was surrounded by mountains sloping down to the sea, flat and
smooth, all elongated, 3000 stadia long (about 555 km or
345 mi) on two sides, and at the center, 2000 stadia (about
370 km or 230 mi) from the sea all the way down. [...] At
a distance of about 50 stadia (9 km or 5.7 mi), there was
a mountain of moderate size on each side [...]. The island,
where the abode of the kings was located, had a diameter
of 5 stadia (a little less than 1 km, about half a mile)." In
Critias, a dialogue that unfortunately was not completed,
Plato furthermore dates the existence of Atlantis to about
11,000 years ago, when Poseidon "enclosed the hill [...] by
alternating three stretches of sea and land in concentric circles of different widths, of which two were land and three
were water." At the center of the capital of Atlantis rose the
imposing temple of Poseidon, all covered with silver, and
housing the majestic statue of the god of the sea and his
chargers, as high as the temple itself, and all golden.

At a distance of over 2000 years, Plato's text triggers fantasies and inspires the greatest treasure hunt in progress on
our planet. Plato is considered a reliable author, his stories
were taken as historical reality, as done by Crantor of Soli,
the first philosopher to provide commentaries on Plato's
works. From that point, the island of Atlantis, vanished
11,000 years earlier, has been imagined and situated almost
everywhere on the planet: from the peaks of the Bolivian
highlands to the depths of the Atlantic Ocean Ridge;
from the glaciers of Antarctica to the warm waters of the
Caribbean. Atlantis is everywhere, like all archetypes that
pass through cultures and peoples distant from one anoth-

er in time and space. But the theory most dear to Plato's descendants situates Atlantis in Greece itself. And in particular, in the archipelago of the Cyclades, at an island that was called Thera in ancient times, today known as Santorini. Santorini is one of the most suggestive islands in the world: its present structure is all that remains after a series of volcanic explosions, the most clamorous of which is said to have devastated the entire Mediterranean Sea. The explosion of Thera hurled about 18 cu km (4.3 cu mi) of magma into the ancient heavens: the dating of artifacts discovered enwrapped within this mortal rain of lava situates the eruption around the year 1456 BC. The same date was hypothesized by geologist Angelos Galanopoulos, who even set the explosive volcano in relation to various events described in the Bible: some earthquakes, the mythical opening of the waters of the Red Sea, and above all, the "three days of darkness" in the Exodus, which would correspond to a sky filled with volcanic ash. The problem is that this date does not coincide with the date of 9000 BC given by Plato. Galanopoulos then imagined the possibility of an error in transcription: if the year were 900 instead of 9000. But the identification with Santorini is just one of the hundreds of hypotheses on which researchers from all nations have been working, sometimes even dedicating their whole lives to this. The hunt for the Lost Continent continues.

THE PALACE
OF KNOSSOS
Greece

*Theseus, Ariadne, Daedalus, and the monstrous
Minotaur: the greatest myths of Greece "dance"
around the ruins of the palace in the heart of Crete.*

Crete is the largest island of Greece, situated in the heart of the Mediterranean Sea. A few kilometers from the capital Heraklion stands a place shrouded in legend: the Palace of Knossos. It is the ancient prison of the mythical Minotaur, the gigantic semi-human creature with the head of a bull.

The Palace of Knossos is a superb testimony of the Minoan civilization that dominated the island of Crete from the third millennium BC. The city-palace dating from the beginning of the 16th century BC was unearthed in 1900 owing to excavations by English archaeologist Arthur Evans, who also organized restorations and reconstructions of its ruined structures, even reproducing their original paintings.

The ancient complex consisted of 1400 rooms spread over an area of 22,000 sq m (5.4 acres). Today one can visit the processional hall, the storerooms with their antique jars, the sanctuary, the royal apartments, and the throne room with its marble seat.

The city-palace of Knossos has given rise to one of the themes in Western culture, one that has led to many reflections in art and literature: the labyrinth.

13th century BC - The Palace of Knossos is abandoned for unknown reasons.

1878 - Minos Kalokairinos, a Cretan merchant, discovers the Palace of Knossos site.

1886 - The German archaeologist Heinrich Schliemann, who discovered Troy, visits Knossos to verify the possibility of undertaking digs.

1900 - The English archaeologist Sir Arthur Evans begins excavation of the Palace, which lasts for the next 35 years.

1905 - Evans finds a stone vase in the shape of a bull's head in the Little Palace zone.

Perhaps the construction of this palace, corresponds to the work conceived by Daedalus, the architect passed down through myth.

There are countless myths connected with the labyrinth, to be found in every culture, in every corner of the planet: it is an archetype that has forever obsessed mankind.

According to some, Knossos Palace could be the labyrinth fashioned to enclose the Minotaur. For others, it might be an enormous temple.

The myth of the Minotaur is closely connected with the history of Crete. The theme of the bull recurs in the frescoes at Knossos and in archaeological finds. It is often represented in scenes where young men and women are shown flipping over the animal's back. Coins found at Knossos depict a labyrinth, at whose center are signs that some have interpreted as the horns of the bull, while others have called them a quarter moon. According to one version of the myth that has many variants, Zeus transformed himself into a bull to abduct Europa, the very beautiful young earthly lady, to take her to Crete; with her he sired three children, one of whom was Minos.

Minos was adopted by the king of Crete and succeeded him upon his death with the help of Poseidon, who helped him to win the competition for the succession by causing a white bull to issue forth from the foam of the sea.

Minos, was overcome by the bull's beauty and refused to sacrifice it as he had promised Poseidon. The God of the Sea took his revenge by causing Minos's wife to fall in love with the bull. The union of the two generated Asterion, known as the Minotaur, with the body of a man and the head of the bull, a bloodthirsty beast that fed upon human flesh. The king charged Daedalus to build a prison suitable for holding the monster: the labyrinth, a maze of twisty narrow spaces from which, once one had entered, it was impossible to find a way out.

The imprisoned Minotaur was fed with young human victims sent from Athens every nine years. But on the third tribute, among the seven youths and seven maidens sent from Athens as predestined victims was the young hero Theseus, who had already defeated the white bull of Poseidon, a source of devastation for Greece. Theseus conquered Ariadne, the daughter of Minos, and with her help (the stratagem of the magic thread allowing him to find the exit to the maze) he entered the labyrinth, killing the Minotaur and freeing the hostages before emerging victorious.

There are some who would read in these myths a reference to the ritual fights the Cretan king performed with animals: a struggle symbolizing the victory of the royal power over nature. On the other hand, the tribute of human sacrifices imposed by Minos upon Athens recalls the historical period of Crete's domination of the Mediterranean. The structure of the palace testifies to the absolute tranquility of a king who had no fears of attacks or invasions from the sea. Dangers could arrive only from within: possibly, from the legendary underground crypt, identified as the prison of the Minotaur, the fearsome monster, imaginary or real as it may have been.

THE PYRAMID
OF KHUFU

Egypt

"Man fears time.
But time fears the pyramids."

Ancient Arab proverb

The pyramid of Khufu (Cheops) is the world's most known and visited monument. It is the only one of the legendary seven wonders of the ancient world that has succeeded in crossing through the centuries to arrive intact to our own time. The monument lies in the outskirts of the modern metropolis of Cairo, on the Giza plateau, right beside the mysterious Sphinx and near two other pyramids of smaller dimensions: those of Khafre (Chephren) and of Menkaure (Mycerinus). Official archaeology sustains that it was constructed as a funereal monument for Pharaoh Khufu of the Fourth Dynasty. But there are many who have imagined and proposed other hypothesis. The fact that the pyramids attributed to the Fourth Dynasty demonstrate a technical level that is incredibly higher with respect to the preceding and, above all, with respect to those following, has aroused numerous debates and more than one suspicion. It is as though in just a few years, technology had passed from that of the printing press to that of the laptop, then reverted to the printing press and movable type: an evolution and involution that are difficult to explain. Supposedly more than

2605 BC - The Fourth Dynasty pharaoh Khufu (Cheops) ascends the throne.

5th century BC - The ancient Greek historian Herodotus describes the Great Pyramid in *The Histories*.

AD 820 - The men in the service of Arab caliph el-Mamun succeed in entering the pyramid by digging a tunnel.

1798 - Napoleon fights against the Mamluks near Giza in the Battle of the Pyramids.

1954 - The Egyptian archaeologist Kamal el-Mallakh finds a pit near the pyramid containing a disassembled wooden boat, which is reassembled the following years.

100,000 people worked to build the pyramid, placing 2.5 million blocks of stone in about 30 years. What were the means used and who were the men that the successive pharaohs of the Fourth Dynasty used to construct their pyramids. Originally, the Pyramid of Khufu was greater than 145 m (475 ft) in height. Today it stands 139 m (455 ft) high and is 230 m (755 ft) wide at the base of each side. The proportions of the monument also denote an incredible level of precision. The lengths of the individual parts differ from one another by only 0.1 percent, and the four faces of the pyramid are aligned with the cardinal points.

Even the position of the pyramid does not seem to have been chosen at random; it rises from the point of intersection between one particular meridian and one particular parallel sharing the same characteristic, that is, they are the lines of their sort covering the greatest amount of dry land, making this point, in fact, the center of the world, at least from the point of view of land mass. There are those who have calculated that its weight (5273 million tonnes) multiplied by a billion billions is equivalent to the weight of the planet. Others have calculated that its dimensions are connected with the value of π (pi), which, however, was discovered many centuries after its construction.

The questions and mysteries surrounding the Pyramid of Khufu did not relate only to who constructed it and to what technique was used. Doubt has been raised about whether it actually was a tomb because no remains of any pharaoh have ever been found inside it. But does it have an operational function? What link does it have to the stars? What secrets does it still conceal within itself?

Inside the monument there are only two rooms: one is bare and unadorned, while the other is called "the king's chamber," which houses the presumed sarcophagus and an inscription based on which archaeologists have attributed the pyramid to Khufu. But that which is believed to be the sarcophagus is empty. And not only that: it was realized and worked from a single block of granite, and it is larger than the access door into the room. Its external volume is exactly twice the internal volume: a precision truly difficult to obtain using the instruments available 5000 years ago.

Archaeologist Flinders Petrie maintains that a similar result could only have been obtained using a circular saw of bronze and diamonds. Engineer Christopher Dunn, an expert in working granite, sustains that in order to realize this sarcophagus today without breaking the block of stone, it would take a drill 500 times faster than those commercially available. The ancient Egyptians must have possessed incredible utensils, of which no trace has been conserved.

Then there are the connections with the sky and the stars. There are some who maintain that the three pyramids of pizza reproduce on earth the three stars of the belt of Orion and their respective arrangement within the sky. According to a fantastical but fascinating hypothesis, the Sphinx would then complete the astral picture, by fixing the position of the constellation Leo in the sky and thus dating the entire archaeological area to 10,500 BC. In the epoch of its maximum splendor, when the Great Pyramid was entirely covered over with white limestone from Tura, it shone for great distances. It has been calculated that it even would have been visible from the moon, in all its unfathomable mystery.

THE SPHINX

Egypt

A human head on the body of a lion,
guarding Egypt's oldest mystery.

The Sphinx at Giza is one of the symbols of Egypt, the enigmatic colossal statue with the body of a lion and the head of man. The interpretation of the mysterious monument right in front of the pyramids of Khufu (Cheops), Khafre (Chephren) and Menkaure (Mycerinus) is controversial. Set at the bottom of a wide and deep pit, the Sphinx is 73 m (240 ft) long, 6 m (19.7 ft) wide, and 20 m (65.6 ft) high. It is the largest statue in the world; majestic and imposing, it has for centuries fascinated travelers, explorers, and archaeologists. Many times the desert sands have tried to bury it, but each time it has reemerged from oblivion. According to official archaeology, its face is the likeness of the Pharaoh Khafre and it was realized around 2500 BC, by liberating its form from the stone that surrounded it. But still no satisfactory explanation has been provided for how the enormous blocks composing it were transported and cut.

And there are some who support the theory that the Sphinx actually dates from a much older time, as far back as 10,500 BC.

This hypothesis is linked to the stars. Carved into the limestone rock and perfectly oriented toward the east, the Sphinx faces the rising sun on the days of the vernal and autumnal equinoxes. In 10,500 BC,

2558 BC - The Fourth Dynasty pharaoh Chephren ascends the throne.

1380 BC - The Thirteenth Dynasty pharaoh Thutmose IV builds, between the paws of the Sphinx, the so-called Dream Stela to commemorate the restoration of the monument.

AD 1378 - The Sphinx's nose is destroyed.

1817 - The Italian Giovanni Battista Caviglia carries out the first modern archeological research after freeing the Sphinx's body from the sand.

the constellation of Leo was exactly on the horizon of Egypt. The Sphinx would thus have been "looking at itself" (its leonine body) being reflected in the firmament. Just as the three pyramids of Giza would have been reflected in the three stars shining in Orion's belt.

But what basis could such a fanciful hypothesis have? Is it really possible that the Sphinx could have been produced many millennia earlier than what the Egyptologists believe? Normally it is believed that the Sphinx was built around 2500 BC, considering that the ancient Egyptians would not have had the technology, the social organization, or perhaps even the capability of constructing such a monument thousands of years earlier than the reign of Khafre. But if the official dating is correct, we need to hypothesize that the visible signs of erosion on the Sphinx and on the rocky walls surrounding it were due only to the action of the wind and perhaps a few extraordinary floods of the Nile. For many researchers, the signs of erosion could be the signs of strong and prolonged rains. And this could only have happened before these areas became desert, when the land of Egypt was green and temperate. The last wet and rainy period of northern Africa dates back to the centuries between 13,000 BC and 10,000 BC, which explains the possibility of dating the Sphinx to a very ancient era.

But the Sphinx also conceals another mystery: does its face actually depict Khafre, or did the pharaoh simply modify the existing head? Furthermore, the head appears to have been made of a stone different from that used for the rest of the body, and above all, it is disproportionate. The ancient Egyptians had an outright obsession for symmetry and proportion: is it possible that they would no longer apply this characteristic of theirs in such an important monument?

Egyptologists attribute the construction of the Sphinx to Khafre, because they maintain that the face resembles the one on a famous black diorite statue portraying the pharaoh. This theory, however, was refuted in the 1990s by Frank Domingo, the forensic science expert of New York, who excluded the possibility of their representing the same face. According to analyses performed and facial composites produced, the two faces would even belong to different races.

Another legend regards the existence of a secret underground chamber beneath the Sphinx, containing extremely old archives. According to the prophetic visions of psychic Edgar Cayce, these would correspond to the legendary "Hall of Documents" of the civilization of Atlantis, which also disappeared, according to the myth, 11,000 years ago.

The only thing certain is that the Sphinx has been maintaining its secrets and fascinating researchers and lovers of mystery for millennia. The truth is probably hidden in its face, which has forever been synonymous with mystery itself.

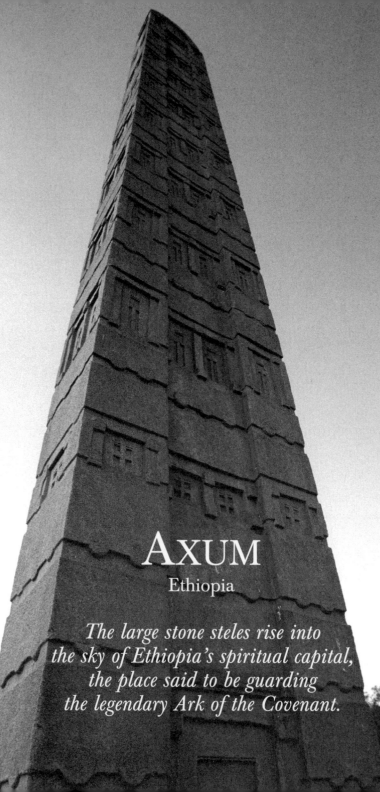

AXUM
Ethiopia

*The large stone steles rise into
the sky of Ethiopia's spiritual capital,
the place said to be guarding
the legendary Ark of the Covenant.*

Ethiopia, on the Horn of Africa, is a land of noble peoples, unique animals, and torrid deserts of lava and salt. Some of the most incomprehensible kingdoms in history have sprung from its red soil. Very wealthy kingdoms that have disappeared into nothingness. Legendary civilizations, like that of the Axumites, who left a series of mysterious traces in their ancient capital of Axum.

The first mention of this mysterious realm appears on an ancient document known as *Periplus Maris Erythraei*: in this travel log, the author describes the kingdom of the *Aksumites* as a rich land governed by the king Zoscales, a cultured dictator who was also an expert in literature, but with expansionist aims. The Axumite civilization reached such a level of sophistication that its people produced gold coins of great value, with images representing likenesses of at least 20 different sovereigns. Rare and precious coins that hint at the history and allure of this ancient African kingdom. According to recent studies, the Axumite civilization dates back at least to the 4th century BC, but its origins have not yet been clarified. To add to the confusion, the ancient official Axumite language of Ge'ez, used by the imperial court of Ethiopia in certain documents up until 1974 and still in use by the

1st century AD - The Axumite Empire is at its acme.

1665 - Our Lady Mary of Zion Church is built at Axum.

1937 - Benito Mussolini's Fascist regime removes the large monument known as the Obelisk of Axum from its original site and transports it to Italy.

1980 - The ruins of Axum are placed on the UNESCO World Heritage List.

2005 - Italy repatriates the Obelisk of Axum to Ethiopia.

Ethiopian Orthodox Church as a liturgical language, dates back as far as 2000 BC.

But there is one characteristic that renders this African civilization truly unique and impressive: the monumental steles constructed from single blocks of granite, which can still be seen by the dozens today in modern Axum: some damaged and on the ground, others standing out with their nearly 30 m (98.4 ft) of height. But their significance still remains a mystery. Among those still standing there is the one known as the stele of King Ezana, 24 m (78.7 ft) high, which since 2008 has been standing side by side with its twin stele, returned by Italy to Ethiopia. But the great stele of Axum, whose collapse, according to legend, marked the end of the Axumite empire, was no less than 33 m (108 ft) high; it still lies today at the point where the gods supposedly caused it to fall. The Axumite steles have only one style: the decorations that embellish it seem to represent doors and windows, at times with ornamentations like handles; they are always concave realizations within the steles themselves, as though they were to host plates or precious images, which, however, no one has ever found.

One wonders about the nature of the steles: it would seem strange for them simply to be funereal monuments because there are no graves around their location. And their style, which is more like that of a home than that of a monument, is a mystery, as is also the existence of what may have been the metal plaques, now vanished. According to certain calculations, the block of stone constituting the Great Stele ought to weigh about 520 tonnes (573 tons). Modern architects and archaeologists still do not clearly understand how it was possible for them to move it for over 4 km (2.5 mi) – the distance from the quarries – and then position it upright.

But the steles are not the only mystery of the ancient Axumite civilization. According to testimonies of several travelers, it would appear that one can feel the ground resonate under one's feet, owing to the incredible numbers of tombs and caves that pierce the area. Certain legends affirm that the dense network of underground vaults, the majority of which are yet unexplored, conceals a passage leading as far as Arabia.

There remains also the mystery of what caused the downfall of the mythical Axumite civilization, the reason for which a people capable of such cultural sophistication and imposing monuments would fall into oblivion. The legends reported in certain texts, jealously guarded by local monks, speak of a warrior queen named Judith, perhaps a pagan or perhaps of Hebrew origin, who in a single night destroyed the city by fire. Judith killed the last Axumite sovereign and knocked down a great number of steles. The only thing that is certain is that the last remaining obelisks, the smallest, without inscriptions, are now conserved in a park dedicated to her. The last intangible traces of a majestic, secret people, buried by the sands of time.

Axum today is a destination of great pilgrimages: it is considered the holiest city in Ethiopia. The Ethiopian Orthodox Church affirms that the Church of Our Lady Mary of Zion conserves the legendary Ark of the Covenant, the tabernacle with supernatural powers containing Moses' Ten Commandments. It is too bad that no one can observe it or touch it other than the guardian of the church – the sole person elected to have this privilege – who guards it day and night for his entire life. But this is just another of the thousand secrets of enigmatic Axum.

LALIBELA

Ethiopia

Splendid churches carved into the rock.
Legends appearing to indicate that the Ark
of the Covenant passed by here centuries ago.

Ethiopia is a mythical land, traversed by a thousand mysteries and legends. At 2600 m (8530 ft) elevation, we find what is called the "Petra of Africa": Lalibela. This is the most sacred city after Axum, and it is famous for its incredible churches excavated into the sides of the mountain, or even into the depths of the earth. There are 10 churches and a small prison; nobody knows how or when they were built. The founding of Lalibela is generally dated to the 12th century, but its origin is probably even older. All the churches were built without any masonry elements or wooden structural parts, but only by excavating and working the tufa rock. Making it all even more mysterious is the fact that, except for the churches, there is no other construction from the same era anywhere in the area.

Legend has it that the shrines were built on the orders of King Lalibela, following a mystical vision that came to him. According to some scholars, 40,000 workmen were needed to build the entire complex by excavating it from the rock; that number, however, is incompatible with the actual population of the area during that historical period. According to another version, the construction of the Christian churches was supervised by knights

c. 1200 - King Lalibela of Ethiopia founds his rock-hewn capital, drawing inspiration from Jerusalem.

1500 - The Portuguese explorer Pero da Covilha is the first European to visit the churches of Lalibela.

c. 1865 - After the period of Portuguese exploration in the 16th-century, the German Friedrich Gerhard Rohlfs is the first European to visit Lalibela again.

1978 - Lalibela is placed on the UNESCO World Heritage List.

of the Crusades who took refuge in Ethiopia. The churches of Lalibela are divided into two distinct areas, with the sole exception of the church dedicated to St. George. The most important group is the one to the northwest, which includes Bet Medhane Alem, "the Church of the Savior," considered the largest monolithic rock-hewn church in the world. In its interior are carved stone niches that are identified – in a totally anachronistic manner – with the tombs of Abraham, Isaac, and Jacob; this is also where Lalibela's most precious treasure, a gigantic cross of gold weighing more than 7 kg (18.75 troy lbs), is conserved. Bet Maryam, "the Church of Maria," is reached by passing through a small stone arch in a wall of rock. The plan is highly elaborate: the interior is realized on two floors, and there are many frescoes representing Christian symbols, but there is also a strange beast with two heads fighting two bulls, one white and one black. Farther on, a column with a square base is covered with drapes and very thick fabrics; it is said that under these is a forbidden inscription, which cannot be viewed by anyone other than one particular priest. According to local guides, its sacred pages contain the truth about the Ark of the Covenant. Ancient, mysterious manuscripts bound in leather and bark are conserved in the tiny churches of Bet Meskel and Bet Danaghel. However, Bet Golgotha is the holiest church for the Ethiopians: entry is forbidden to women, and on its walls are frescoes of crusader warriors in fighting gear.

The priest also serves as guard for a series of relics, but above all, for a small corner of earth considered holy.

The second group of churches, the one to the southeast, is poorly conserved and difficult to access. Only the tiny prison, with its shackles and chains, raises several questions: who would have been locked up in a site containing only places of worship?

But the most astonishing church at Lalibela is doubtlessly Bet Giyorgis, realized by excavating 15 m (50 ft) deep into the rocky base of the hill. Dedicated to St. George and based on a cruciform plan, it develops over three floors of depth. Today it still hosts mystical hermits, who live half naked in its sacred niches side-by-side with skeletons that have been deposited there over the centuries. An antique chest and other sealed boxes conserved there are never opened before strangers and no one knows what they contain. Other marks in the rocks are attributed to the hooves of St. George's horse, which manifested to reveal to the saint a secret that remains well-guarded in the depths of the earth.

THE RUINS OF GEDI

Kenya

A city forgotten in the forest of Kenya seems to be shrouded by an ancient curse and a fascinating history.

Malindi, in Kenya, today is considered one of the paradises of Africa. Its dreamlike coast along eastern Africa is a destination for the most sophisticated tourism. And yet, a few miles from its exclusive dwellings, there is a mysterious little village, a ghost town with an uncertain past: the Gedi Ruins, the lost village. *Gede* means "precious" in the Oromo language. Embedded within the heart of the forest of Arabuko Sokoke, and distributed over 200,000 sq m (50 ac), the ruins of Gedi represent a yet unsolved mystery: nobody knows the earliest history of the village, that of its inhabitants, or the reasons leading to their sudden abandonment. No sign of battle or epidemic has been discovered: the ruins appear, rather, to suggest a rapid flight of the inhabitants. Locals seem to avoid these impenetrable ruins, perhaps because they fear what happened in this ancient and mysterious place.

The crux of the entire enigma surrounding the city lost in the forest is that there are no written traces of its existence: there is no record of it in the Swahili culture; the Portuguese who came to this area and settled just a few miles away did not know about it; the Arab libraries hold no key for deciphering its mystery. The ruins of Gedi appear to have escaped centuries of history with a sort of well-guarded secret.

1884 - Sir John Kirk, the British Consul in Zanzibar, visits the ruins of Gedi for the first time.

1927 - The ruins of Gedi are officially declared a historic monument.

1948 - After being restored, the ruins become a national park.

1958 - The English archaeologist James Kirkman ends the first ten-year archaeological excavation campaign at the Gedi site.

The campaign of excavations conducted between 1948 and 1958 produced surprising results. Hidden among the ruins, archaeologists discovered precious and unexpected valuables: a Chinese vase from the Ming dynasty, precious wrought glass from Venice, an iron lamp of Indian make, scissors from Spain, and coins from the Far East. All these objects have been on display since 2000 in the small museum at the Gedi complex, and appear to relate the story of a place where merchants and travelers from every part of the planet came together in the past. A rich, pulsating, and vital center of Eastern Africa under the Arab rule flourishing between 1300 and 1700 AD. Archaeologists estimate the city was home to at least 2500 inhabitants.

The simplest hypothesis advanced by scholars is that, during the migrations of the tribes that descended from the north, the great forest of Arabuko Sokoke became a destination to be conquered, and its inhabitants were thus brutally driven out. According to another version, however, the city of Gedi was the subject of a punitive expedition launched by the city of Mombasa against Malindi.

But all this only adds to the great mystery of the silence that has surrounded the ruins for centuries: how was it possible for such a rich center of commerce, such an extensive city, where great and powerful merchants of the past converged, not to have left any written trace in any travel log? We would almost have to imagine a pact of silence required to be kept by anyone venturing into the ancient Gedi village. Furthermore, its distance from the sea and its position within the forest are not ideal conditions for a center of commerce. And what further deepens the mystery are questions about *what* the inhabitants of Gedi so secretly traded and *who* their actual customers were.

What remains to be admired today is the typical medieval Swahili architecture that found its culmination in the construction of the palace, the imposing stone homes, and the great mosque. But the sophisticated toilets, unique of their kind, arouse great interest: the primary material used in the construction comes from the coral reef in the nearby ocean. The plan of the city develops upon right-angled intersections and includes an outstanding network of street drains. According to legend, the ruins are protected by the spirits of their priests. The "Old Ones," as they are called, are said to be capable of cursing anyone who attempts to desecrate the area.

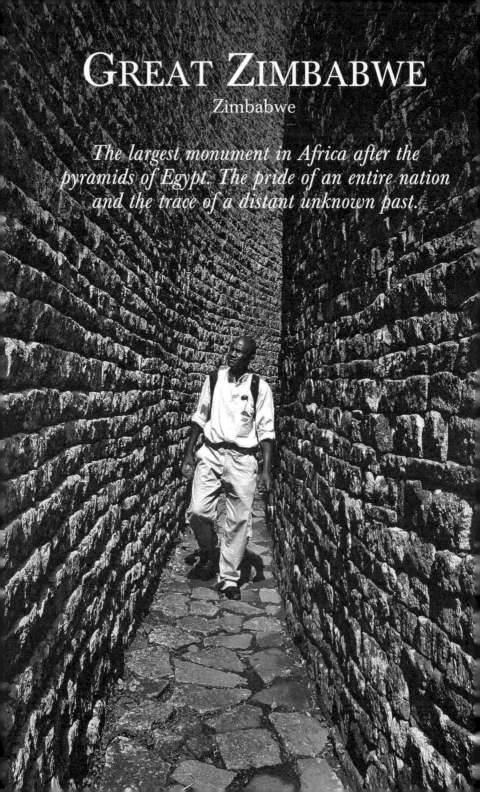

GREAT ZIMBABWE

Zimbabwe

*The largest monument in Africa after the
pyramids of Egypt. The pride of an entire nation
and the trace of a distant unknown past.*

On the continent of Africa, the second monument in size and importance after the pyramids of Egypt is Great Zimbabwe. And just like the pyramids, it has become the symbol of the land of the pharaohs. Accordingly, this spectacular archaeological site has become the icon of the Republic of Zimbabwe, a state that derives its name from the incredible stone ruins overlooking the endless high-lying plateau of Harare. The symbolic bird of the nation – according to some it would be the Bateleur eagle – is one of the most famous finds discovered in the Great Zimbabwe excavations.

The whole place is shrouded in mystery: it was the capital of an empire, extending over 7 sq km (2.7 sq mi), constructed with 15,000 tonnes of stone, forming a series of majestic buildings and imposing walls. Why was Great Zimbabwe abandoned?

Official archaeological dating indicates human presence in the area beginning from the 4th century AD, but clearly states that construction of the magnificent city began only 1000 years later, toward the end of the 13th century. At the height of its splendor, it must have housed more than 20,000 inhabitants: a true capital, with fre-

6th century - Portuguese merchants spread the news of an ancient city in ruins connected with gold mining.

1867 - While on a hunt, Adam Renders rediscovers the ruins of Great Zimbabwe.

1871 - The German explorer and geographer Karl Mauch carries out the first studies of Great Zimbabwe, and even draws a parallel between it and the Temple of Solomon.

1986 - Great Zimbabwe is placed on the UNESCO World Heritage List.

netic traffic and rich with commerce, frequented by Arabs, Indians, and Portuguese. The pulsing heart of the realm of Monomotapa, the legendary Bantu monarch of southeastern Africa.

Great Zimbabwe was inexplicably abandoned and forgotten for centuries, until it was accidentally discovered in 1867 by the explorer Adam Renders. In 1871, German geologist Karl Mauch effected the first reconnaissance and came to establish – erring dramatically – that it was "a copy of the Temple of Solomon and a copy of the palace of the Queen of Sheba." It was not until the early 20th century, with scientific studies not conditioned by racist ideologies, that it was discovered that this spectacular complex was the work of an ancient African people, probably the Shona, even though the Venda and the Lemba claimed to have constructed it: one of the clans of these latter people, in fact, call themselves *Tovakare Muzimbabwe*, "the ones who built Zimbabwe." The name Zimbabwe itself would derive from a contraction of the phrase *dzimba woye*, "the idolized houses." Surrounded by imposing walls, in Great Zimbabwe many stone houses still stand around the city's two great monumental towers (those of mud have been lost), forming narrow passageways among the immense walls of rock. In the highest part of the city (over 2500 m, or 8200 ft, above sea level) we find the Great Enclosure – the largest prehistoric structure south of the Sahara – and the Conical Tower, a masterpiece of design over 9 m (30 ft) high and more than 5 m (16 ft) wide, perhaps the ancient residence of the king. Who were the architects who designed all of this? And after having constructed this enchanting and monumental city of stone, why were the inhabitants constrained to abandon it, leaving it to fall into oblivion for 400 years? The answers seem to remain buried, even today, among its incredibly breathtaking ruins.

NOAH'S ARK
Turkey

*On the summit of Mount Ararat, in search
of evidence confirming the most ancient of legends.*

With its elevation of 5165 m (16,945 ft), Mount Ararat dominates the scenery and culture of the entire region of Kurdistan near Turkey. Its profile appears in the center of the emblem of the Republic of Armenia, for whose people the mountain is sacred. But for the rest of the world, Mount Ararat is simply the mountain at the top of which Noah landed, according to the Bible, after the Great Flood.

In certain photographs, which by now have become famous, one can see a strange, unidentified object called "the Ararat anomaly" at the northwest crest. Many researchers believe this could be the remains of the legendary Ark, but so far the Turkish government has denied scientific expeditions access to the peak, declaring the zone to be a military area.

The myth of Ararat comes from the book of Genesis, where we read: "The Lord then said to Noah, 'Go into the ark, you and your whole family, because I have found you righteous in this generation. Take with you seven pairs of every kind of clean animal, a male and its mate [...] Seven days from now I will send rain on the earth for 40 days and 40 nights; and I will wipe from the face of the

2370 BC - According to tradition, this was the year the Great Flood supposedly occurred.

c. AD 1300 - In his *Travels* Marco Polo mentions Mt. Ararat as the place where Noah's Ark landed.

1840 - A violent earthquake strikes Mt. Ararat.

2012 - The Dutch millionaire Johan Huibers builds a full-sized replica of Noah's Ark as described in the Old Testament; it is in Dordrecht, Holland and is open to the public.

earth every living creature I have made.' And Noah did all that the Lord commanded him." (Genesis 7:1).

According to the Bible, the water covered the entire surface of the earth. The highest mountain was covered over by fully 15 cubits – about 7 m (22.9 ft) – and supposedly all this happened around 2370 BC.

The myth of such a global catastrophe is present in the legends of many peoples who are very different and remotely located from one another. The name of Noah is known in many regions of the world: in Amazonia, he is identified as Noa; the Hawaiians call him Nu-u; the Chinese recognize him as Nuwah; and in Mexico, there exists a Nalá. But the legend is even widespread in civilizations that have never come into contact with one another: there are over 150 known stories of the Flood. Even the Mesopotamian epic of Gilgamesh relates a story of the Flood highly similar to that found in the Bible: Tutu is asked to tear down his house in order to build an ark and save himself.

Scholars have attempted to reconstruct Noah's ark. At Dordrecht, in Holland, Joan Huibers built a life-size copy of the ark, following the indications given in Genesis: "So make yourself an ark of cypress wood; make rooms in it and coat it with pitch inside and out. This is how you are to build it: The ark is to be three hundred cubits long, fifty cubits wide, and thirty cubits high. Make a roof for it, leaving below the roof an opening one cubit high all around. Put a door in the side of the ark and make lower, middle and upper decks." (Genesis 6, 14-16).

The result, in fact, is a parallelepiped 156 m (171 yds) long, 26 m (28.4 yds) wide, and over 15 m (50 ft) high. An enormous crate, longer than a soccer field and as high as a four-story building, with neither bow nor stern, nor even a rudder. But he acquitted his task, according to legend: "But God remembered Noah and all the wild animals and the livestock that were with him in the ark, and he sent a wind over the earth, and the waters receded. Now the springs of the deep and the floodgates of the heavens had been closed, and the rain had stopped falling from the sky. The water receded steadily from the earth. At the end of the hundred and fifty days the water had gone down, and on the seventeenth day of the seventh month the ark came to rest on the mountains of Ararat." (Genesis 8, 1-4).

The Bible text speaks of mountains in the plural: in effect the Ararat massif is divided into the Great Ararat and the Little Ararat, two mountains separated about 11 km (6.8 mi). By combining all the information we can establish that Noah ought to have landed at about 800 m (2625 ft) from the summit, at 4365 m (14,320 ft) elevation. In 1840, a massive volcanic explosion involved part of Ararat: at that point the wood of the legendary ark could possibly have slipped downhill. Or it might have been lost forever. At any rate, the research continues.

GÖBEKLI TEPE

Turkey

The oldest temple in the world is located in Turkey, seeming to want to tell a different story about the origins of civilization.

In southern Turkey, a short distance from the Syrian border, there is a hill that is home to what is called "the most ancient temple in the world," Göbekli Tepe. About 11,000 years ago, the local inhabitants scanned lands of the Mesopotamia and erected mysterious and colossal monuments in honor of gods whose names have long since been forgotten. The discovery of this incredible manmade hill realized 9000 years before Christ, the excavation of which began only in 1994, has constrained us to rewrite the history books: Neolithic men were not, as was believed, merely hunters who lived in caves frescoed by rude graffiti, but instead were capable of constructing places of worship using refined techniques, including the polishing and carving of huge blocks of stone.

At Göbekli Tepe, a series of mysterious columns have been brought to light, produced according to a particular and unusual form, that of a *T*. Some of these reach heights of 6 m (20 ft) and weigh more than 10 tonnes: according to archaeologists' estimates, there are probably 50 throughout the area, and their form could be a stylization of gigantic man.

One wonders how it could have been possible, 3000 years before the invention of writing, for

1963 - A Turkish-American research team surveys the Göbekli Tepe site and discovers traces of a Neolithic culture.

1994 - The German archaeologist Klaus Schmidt begins excavations at the Göbekli Tepe site.

2010 - The Global Heritage Fund announces a ten-year conservation plan for the Göbekli Tepe site.

2014 - Klaus Schmidt, the archaeologist whose name is synonymous with Göbekli Tepe, dies.

the inhabitants of Göbekli Tepe to conceive, design, and build an entire artificial hill, 15 m (50 ft) high and with a diameter reaching 300 m (984 ft), to render homage to their gods. The purpose of the large terraces and numerous stone circles that have been discovered remains unclear. Not to mention the mystery surrounding the remarkable number of bas-reliefs and sculptures depicting plants and animals of every type (for example, serpents, lions, scorpions, boars and bulls), as well as faceless anthropomorphic figures, and the beings worshipped by the ancient inhabitants of Göbekli Tepe, to whom they dedicated statues representing them as winged men.

Some believe that they were ancient shamans, while others see a relationship to the origin of the myth of angels, and still others hypothesize a link with "the legend of the guardians" cited in the Book of Enoch: according to this ancient apocryphal text, the "guardians," superior beings descended from heaven, gave the people of ancient Mesopotamia the secret knowledge of art and science, before disappearing. Another fantastic hypothesis would identify this as the hill-sanctuary of the biblical Eden: various philological studies seem, in fact, to suggest an exciting parallel between the places described in the Bible and the geographic structure and climate of the Turkish site as it must have appeared thousands of years ago.

But beyond the fantasies, the puzzle of Göbekli Tepe still seems far from a solution. The very existence of the temple is in ill agreement with an epoch in which there existed no other human civilization capable of realizing a megalithic monumental work.

Jericho, considered the most ancient city in the world, was constructed 1000 years after Göbekli Tepe, while the megalithic site of Stonehenge was constructed fully 5000 years later. For centuries, the knowledge achieved by the founders of Göbekli Tepe seems to have disappeared into nothingness.

Moreover, the sacred hill seems to have been suddenly abandoned around 8000 BC and carefully covered over with a layer of stone and earth, of an estimated volume ranging from 300 to 500 cu m (10,595 to 22,955 cu ft). Was the discovery, millennia later, really just a stroke of fortune, or is it possible that those men from very ancient times, equipped with knowledge superior to those of their own time, had sought to preserve this sacred site so that it would endure to our own days?

All the answers appear still to be buried underground. According to geo-radar and geomagnetic surveys, at least 16 more megalithic rings are buried in the 22 ha (54.4 acres) of surrounding land. And as Klaus Schmidt, the archaeologist who directed the works in Turkey, stated, only 5 percent of the site has thus far been excavated; scholars could excavate for another 50 years and succeed in only barely scratching the surface. The mystery of the world's oldest temple will surely engage more than one generation of archaeologists.

HAR MEGIDDO

Israel

*According to the sacred texts, the last battle
of mankind will be fought on a mountain
in Israel. And it will be Armageddon.*

I f the Carmelo Ridge is peaking to your left, and on your right is the crest of Mount Gilboa, and to your back you have the Samaria region, and before you, the valley leading to Nazareth, you are probably standing on top of one of the most spiritual places on our planet: to be sure, you are right in the middle of Armageddon. The name Armageddon has become popular owing to millennial fears and big Hollywood productions: it is, in fact, synonymous with the end of the world. No one knows how and when it will arrive, but ancient sacred texts indicate its location precisely: it will take place on Mount Megiddo (in ancient Hebrew, *Har Megiddo*, whence derives the modern term Armageddon). This is the place where, according to the New Testament Book of Revelation, the final battle between all the kings of the earth will take place, between the forces of good, guided by Christ, and those of evil, incited by Satan.

But what is so special about this hill in the heart of Israel? The city state of Megiddo is mentioned several times in the Bible, and also in relation to important figures such as Joshua, Solomon, and Josiah. Inhabited for more than 6000 years —

1478 BC - The most ancient battle ever documented takes place at Megiddo, fought between the army of Egyptian pharaoh Thutmose III and a Canaanite coalition.

1903 - The American archaeologist Gottlieb Schumacher carries out the first excavations at Megiddo.

1914 - The British Army, headed by General Allenby, fights against the Ottoman army near Megiddo during World War One.

2005 - At Megiddo, the Israeli archaeologist Yotam Tepper discovers the remains of what may be the oldest Christian church in the world.

from 7000 BC to 500 BC – Megiddo was at the center of the economic and political routes of antiquity, an obligatory stop on the road that linked Egypt to Mesopotamia. As such, the city had great strategic importance.

Mount Megiddo, in particular, is a hill of debris that tells the incredible story of at least 25 civilizations that have succeeded one another over the course of their millennial history. The archaeological layers of Megiddo are a priceless treasure of knowledge: every square yard of earth is a page of a book, yet to be deciphered. A tale steeped in the blood of many armies, who clashed and fought right at Megiddo.

The place that seems destined to be the theater of the final battle of humanity appears already to have known many wars throughout its history. The most recent was during the World War One, when the British and Ottoman armies faced off at Megiddo. The British victory marked the definitive retreat of the Turks from the Middle East after more than five centuries of domination.

Many centuries earlier, in 609 BC, Egyptian soldiers guided by Pharaoh Necho II had the better of the people of Judea, led by King Josiah. The sovereign himself was killed, and ever since that time, in the Jewish culture, the battle of Megiddo has been synonymous with absolute ruin.

But the most famous of the conflicts fought around this hill saw the troops of Pharaoh Thutmose III opposing the people of Canaan in 1478 BC. This is the most ancient battle for which we have historical testimony, document- ed in the hieroglyphics carved in the temple of Karnak. It was a very long siege, resolved, according to legend, by a mysterious and magical "weapon of light" possessed by the Egyptians.

The immense doors that resisted the pharaoh's fury for months still dominate the city; the higher ones are said to have been constructed by the legendary King Solomon. Another sacred place is the huge round altar for sacrificial offerings. Also suggestive are the 180 steps leading toward the ancient tunnels constructed during the reign of Ahab.

But the complete secrets of Megiddo are yet to be deciphered. Suffice it to say that in this area it was only in 2005 that the remains were found of a mosaic belonging to what may be the oldest Christian church in the world. Excavations continue, delving for the truth about Armageddon. Which here is, fortunately, still only the name of a mountain.

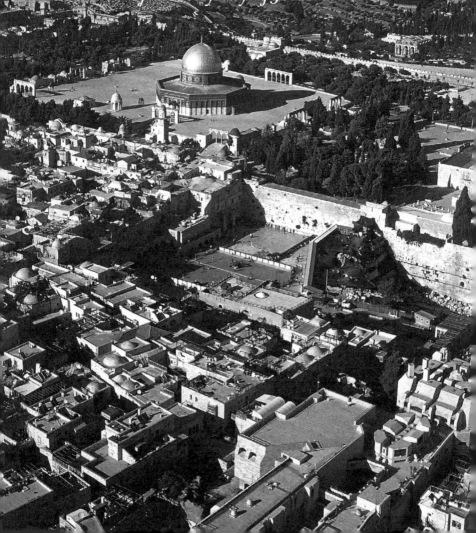

THE TEMPLE OF KING SOLOMON

Israel

*The most precious treasure is perhaps hidden
in the most sacred heart
of the holy city of Jerusalem.*

The construction of the Temple of Solomon began, according to the Bible, in 833 BC, and was completed seven years later. To demonstrate the importance of this building, we need only consider that of the 11 chapters dedicated to the figure of Solomon – third king of Israel, after Saul and David – in the Book of Kings of the Bible, more than three deal with the history of the construction of the legendary temple.

Yahweh revealed to King David, the father of Solomon: "But I have chosen Jerusalem, that my name might be there ..." (II Chronicles 6:6). The sovereign had thus planned to build a temple and Solomon, his son and successor, realized this project. The temple, the earthly seat of Yahweh, conserved within itself the Ark of the Covenant, the fabled chest of acacia wood overlaid with gold that God had caused Moses to build, to conserve "... a golden jar holding the manna, and Aaron's rod which budded, and the tables of the covenant ..." (Hebrews 9:4).

The Ark had already been transported to Jerusalem according to the will of David, with the intention of making Jerusalem the new religious as well as political capital of the new Kingdom of Israel. King Solomon, who had become famous for his wisdom (when Yahweh appeared to him in a dream and promised to fulfill his wish, Solomon did not ask for long life or wealth, but "an understanding heart to judge Your people to discern between good and evil." I Kings 3:9). During his very long reign (970 to

833 BC - Construction of the Temple of Solomon begins.

587 BC - The Babylonian king Nebuchadnezzar II destroys the temple.

516 BC - The second Temple of Jerusalem is consecrated.

AD 70 - Roman emperor Titus razes the Second Temple of Jerusalem to the ground.

930 BC), he strengthened the process of unification and built the temple that would serve as national shrine. Inside would be hidden the greatest treasure of all time.

Based on the indications of the biblical texts, the structure of the temple was tripartite: a vestibular area, a central hall, and within it the *debir* – the Holy of Holies containing the Ark of the Covenant. The temple was erected on the outskirts of the city of David and dominated the city from above. In the open space before it rose the sacrificial altar. According to the description of the Old Testament (I Kings 6), the temple was about 30 m (98 ft) long, 10 m (33 ft) wide, and 15 m (50 ft) high; it was built of stone, covered entirely with cedar wood, carved with rosettes and flower buds. But the most important part was obviously its sanctuary, filled with treasures and relics: Solomon "prepared the inner sanctuary within the temple to set the Ark of the Covenant of the Lord there. The inner sanctuary was twenty cubits long, twenty wide and twenty high. He overlaid the inside with pure gold, and he also overlaid the altar of cedar. Solomon covered the inside of the temple with pure gold, and he extended gold chains across the front of the inner sanctuary, which was overlaid with gold. So he overlaid the whole interior with gold. He also overlaid with gold the altar that belonged to the inner sanctuary. For the inner sanctuary he made a pair of cherubim out of olive wood, each ten cubits high." (I Kings 6).

After the solemn placement of the Ark in the sanctuary, a cloud filled the temple, a sign of the divine presence, and Solomon inaugurated the sacred building with a solemn ceremony and a sacrifice of no fewer than 22,000 oxen and 120,000 sheep. Upon Solomon's death, however, the unity of the kingdom of Israel broke and in 587 BC, King Nebuchadnezzar of the Babylonians had the temple razed. A second temple was constructed 40 years later, but this was definitively destroyed by the Roman emperor Titus in 70 AD.

The only thing remaining from the legendary temple is part of a western retaining wall, what is now known as the famous Wailing Wall. The place where even today, thousands of years later, Solomon's descendants mourn the destruction of the legendary temple.

But perhaps the greatest mystery is that of the disappearance of the Ark of the Covenant. Many think it was hidden by the Knights Templar in some safe place in Europe. According to another legendary version, however, the Ark was given by King Solomon to Menelik, the son born from his relationship with the queen of Sheba, and first Emperor of Ethiopia, where even today the priests of Axum affirm that they are guarding the Ark.

But there also exists a third hypothesis. There are some who maintain, instead, that Solomon had built a hiding place under the shrine, where the Ark was concealed before the Babylonians destroyed the shrine. What is certain is that in the biblical description of the destruction of the Temple and in the detailed report of the plundered booty, the Ark is not mentioned. Some believe it is still located underground, in the area of Jerusalem where the first temple was built, deftly hidden by wise King Solomon. There are two different hypotheses about the actual position of this, the most highly accredited being that it was built on the east hill of the esplanade of the mosques. But in view of the extreme sacredness of the area, holy to three religions, the possibility of excavating there in search of the truth is nothing more than a splendid dream.

THE DEAD SEA SCROLLS
Israel

*A sensational discovery that occurred
within a series of abandoned caves
in the desert of Israel.*

No place in the world has the same density of history and spirituality as Jerusalem: sacred to three religions, it has forever been the center of conflict. The secrets of its temples are timeless, but about 100 km (60 mi) farther south, in what is now known as the West Bank, in the Valley of Qumran, after centuries of neglect an incredible secret has come to light. A secret that has to do with the origin of Christianity itself.

In 1947, the ancient caves of Qumran were part of Palestine, a territory under British mandate. The caves, abandoned, were used as shelter in the rocky desert scorched by the torrid heat, not far from the salty waters of the Dead Sea. Only a few groups of shepherds or Bedouins trod those inhospitable lands. One of those, the young Mohammed el-Hamed, was playing with his companions, throwing stones, when a muffled sound coming from the depths of a cave revealed a treasure the scale of which he was unable to comprehend: dozens of jars containing scrolls written in ancient languages, words that neither he nor any of his friends were capable of understanding. These were the legendary Dead Sea scrolls, sacred and extremely important texts: the most ancient transcriptions ever found of the Hebrew Bible. The

150 BC - The Essenes settle in the zone of Qumran.

1947 - A shepherd finds the first Dead Sea Scrolls in a cave at Qumran.

1956 - In cave 11 at Qumran, archaeologists discover the last fragment of the Scrolls found to date.

1965 - The Shrine of the Book, the wing of the Israel Museum where the Dead Sea Scrolls are on display, is inaugurated in Jerusalem.

following year, the news was spread to the rest of the world, but the beginning of what was to become the Arab-Israeli war slowed the recovery operation, which lasted until 1956. Eleven caves, over 800 manuscripts, nearly 15,000 fragments: a titanic work to put everything together again.

Experts from every nation worked on it, but the majority of the discoveries were kept secret. What was written there that was not supposed to be known? According to the most fantastical theories, for example, those forming the basis of the bestseller *The Da Vinci Code*, not all of the Gospels have come down to us: those that related the true history of the Holy Grail, instead, were hidden for centuries. And at Qumran they resurfaced.

Today nearly all the Qumran fragments have been published, and they do not include apocryphal Gospels. The most important are visible in the splendid Israel Museum of Jerusalem, where they are conserved at a constant low temperature, shielded from harsh light and atmospheric agents, enclosed within a structure capable of resisting even a nuclear attack, and in a form recalling that of the jars in which the scrolls were found.

The historical and theological disputes about the findings call into question the mysterious sect of the Essenes, who inhabited Qumran between 150 BC and 68 AD: a Jewish community that could have drafted the texts that were found, and could also have possessed initiatory and prophetic knowledge.

The attention of treasure hunters, however, concentrates on one particular fragment discovered in the Qumran caves, the fragment catalogued as 3Q15. By contrast with all the other Qumran scrolls, this fragment is made of copper, perhaps because it had more value than the others. It is a list of 64 locations in which treasures have been concealed. Today many of the names cited on fragment 3Q15 no longer exist, which makes it difficult to orient oneself and follow this ancient treasure map. The only location that still conserves its ancient name is the mausoleum of Av Solom, located at the foot of the Mount of Olives. The copper fragment reads: "Eight talents of silver can be found by digging under the western side of the mausoleum of Av Solom. Seventeen talents are hidden under the water basin at the base of the baths. Gold and baskets of offerings are in this basin, at its four corners."

An attempt is being made to identify the other 63 hiding places indicated on fragment 3Q15, to try to understand what relics they may conceal. Many think it may be the legendary treasure of the Temple of King Solomon, razed to the ground by Roman soldiers under Titus in 70 AD: the treasure could have been stolen, scattered, and hidden all around the area of Jerusalem. Could the manuscripts be the key to finding it?

PETRA, THE LOST CITY

Jordan

*"Match me such marvel save in Eastern clime,
A rose-red city half as old as time."*

John William Burgon

In Jordan, at the edge of the spectacular red desert of Wadi Rum, centuries of time have concealed a thrilling mystery connected to a secret past, to a vanished kingdom and a treasure never found. They call it the City of Tombs, the Pink City, the Lost City, or more simply, Petra.

An entire monumental city carved into the rock, Petra was declared in July 2007 to be one of the New Seven Wonders of the World, but its beauty dates back to a very distant time.

In the 6th century BC, a mysterious nomadic people, the Nabataeans, took control of Petra and turned it into a major commercial hub. The Nabataeans were wealthy and cultivated, but almost all of their original documents have been lost. How was it possible for such an advanced people not to want to leave any trace of themselves?

At its maximum splendor, Petra counted a population of over 20,000. Then, inexplicably, in 106 AD, Petra allowed itself to be annexed by the Roman empire. During the first Crusade, Petra was occupied by King Baldwin I of Jerusalem, and it remained in the hands of Christians until 1187, when Saladin definitively defeated the Christian kingdoms. The last reference to the city appears in the chronicles from 1276 of the sultan Baibars al-Bunduqdari,

1st century BC - The apogee of the Nabataean city of Petra.

AD 106 - Petra falls under Roman dominion.

1812 - The Swiss explorer Johann Ludwig Burckhardt is the first European in centuries to visit the city.

1985 - The city of Petra is placed on the UNESCO World Heritage List.

2007 - A world-wide vote establishes that Petra be listed as one of the New Seven Wonders of the World.

after which the name of this fabulous city fell into oblivion. Such a silence and disappearance from the chronicles is unusual for a capital of the kingdom that at one time was very wealthy.

But if today it is possible for us to visit Petra, we owe this to the courage of the young Swiss adventurer Johann Ludwig Burckhardt. In 1812 he disguised himself as an Arab pilgrim and succeeded in having himself guided to the secret passage that today still marks the entrance to the stone canyon, over 1 km long, leading to Petra.

The first building one encounters on coming out of the canyon is El-Khazneh, "The Treasury": legend has it that a pharaoh at war with the Israelites hid his wealth in the urn that dominates the façade, 43 m (141 ft) high and 30 m (98 ft) wide. The Hollywood film *Indiana Jones and the Last Crusade* gives the impression that the Holy Grail was concealed in this very edifice carved into the rock. But beyond the fantasy, in the 12th century the Crusaders built fully five castles (one of which has yet to be found). Many believe that it was not by chance that Petra fell into oblivion after the fall of the Crusades. Was it simply destiny? Or was there something that needed to remain secret and well-guarded at Petra?

Whether or not a hidden treasure ever existed, the forgotten city certainly was unmatched in wealth.

The Avenue of the Façades is home to the monumental, breathtaking Royal Tombs and the Roman Theater (constructed by the Nabataeans) that seated nearly 3000 persons, arranged in three sections over 45 rows. What spectacles these public crowds may have viewed there is still unknown.

Dominating the whole area there is also a fascinating and

frightening place, called "the Altar of Sacrifices": its polished platform and the channels for allowing the blood to run off make this the world's best conserved sacrificial site. The two obelisks, 7 m (23 ft) tall, represent the totems sacred to Dushara and Al-'Uzza, the divinities worshipped by the Nabataeans, who required blood tributes. Here access was forbidden to ordinary mortals.

But even more impressive is the place called "the Monastery." To reach it, one must face 800 long steps over a steep drop. After arriving to the top, one is in the presence of a colossal edifice carved into the rock, 50 m (164 ft) wide and 45 m (148 ft) high. Possibly the tomb of the Nabataean King Obodas I originally, the Monastery owes its name to the crosses sculpted in its interior, and to a miracle. The conversion of the people of Petra to Christianity was marked by a supernatural event: in the year 423 AD, the Syrian monk Barsauma arrived in Petra and found a people afflicted by four years of drought. The monk kneeled and prayed: immediately a torrential tempest emptied itself upon Petra, resulting in the conversion of the inhabitants to the faith of Christ.

According to archaeologists working at Petra, the enchanting pink city represents barely 15 percent of what might be found still underground. An essay performed right beneath El-Khazneh, in fact, shows an entire underground level of magnitude equal to that which is already apparent. It is as though there were another Petra underneath Petra. Still waiting to be discovered.

MOHENJO-DARO
Pakistan

On the border between India and Pakistan, the ruins of an ancient city seem to testify to an incredible battle that took place in the skies.

I In 1922 near the current border between India and Pakistan, an exceptional archaeological discovery brought to light the remains of an evolved and unknown civilization, which was given the name "Indus Valley civilization" after the great river flowing nearby. But it is also known as the Harappan civilization in reference to another ancient archaeological site discovered in the region. The city unearthed in 1922 was well-conserved and guarded an incredible secret, still waiting to be discovered. Its name is Mohenjo-daro, "the Mountain of the Dead."

According to archaeologists, the city was built around 3000 BC upon an area of 1 sq km (0.4 sq mi), and could accommodate at least 70,000 persons – a true metropolis for the time. The plan of the city reveals a clear urban design: those who built Mohenjo-daro equipped it with a wonderful water system, a perfect drainage system, and a system for heating and ventilation.

The upper part houses the famous Great Bath, two temples, and a granary, while the lower part is dense with dwellings nestled in the series of city blocks that were traced out with geometric precision within the grid of streets. Also found were shops, workshops, and

1922 - Archaeologists discover the ruins of ancient Mohenjo-daro in the Indus Valley.

1979 - Publication of David Davenport's book *Atomic Destruction in 2000 BC*, which propounds the theory that the city was destroyed by a nuclear explosion.

1980 - Mohenjo-daro is placed on the UNESCO World Heritage List.

2012 - Pakistani archaeologists announce that if exceptional measures are not effected, the ruins of Mohenj-daro run the risk of disappearing by 2030.

products bearing inscriptions composed of over 400 different characters, which no one has yet been able to decipher. This evolved and unknown civilization was perhaps the one referred to by the Vedas, the ancient sacred texts of the Hindu religion, when they described a magnificent, advanced, nonviolent society living on the shores of the River Sarasvati.

Around 1500 BC, however, the Harappan civilization disappeared. Mohenjo-daro itself was abandoned. Academic hypotheses about why this occurred point to the changing of the courses of water that supplied the city. Other scholars have considered it possibly related to excessive overpopulation: upon reaching 400,000 inhabitants, the city would have collapsed. Still others consider the possibility of an invasion by the Ari in their destructive campaign of conquest made in honor of the god Indra, "the destroyer of forts."

But there is also another fantastical and incredible hypothesis, one that smacks of science fiction. In 1979, the Sanskrit scholar David Davenport published the book *Atomic Destruction in 2000 BC*. According to the theory proposed in the volume, Mohenjo-daro was destroyed with incredible violence. Analyses performed by experts from the University of Rome show how the bracelets, amphorae, and vitrified stones were all exposed in the past by a wave of heat having a temperature equal to about 1500 °C (2372 °F). The exhibited type of fusion with crystallization is compatible with a nuclear explosion or the impact of a meteor. Furthermore, few skeletons were found after what must have been a dramatic end. And yet laboratory analysis has shown that these, like the stones of the area, are radioactive: the levels of uranium and plutonium registered are absolutely beyond normal. According to Davenport, thousands of years ago, an atomic war was fought in the skies over the Indus Valley; perhaps it was actually fought using the famous "Vimana" cited in sacred Indian texts such as the Vedas and the Puranas. In these texts, it is written that the gods used the Vimana, meaning flying chariots, in combat.

In the epic poem *Ramayana*, we can read the following descriptions: "That chariot moves by itself, all shining and painted ... as it flies it emits a melodious sound that seems like a murmur." Or further: "Suddenly there came a great wind that caused the mountains to shake, and one could see a flame of fire that navigated through the air." In another great Hindu poem, the *Mahabharata*, it is written: "We saw in the sky ... an enormously dark Vimana, which launched flaming projectiles. It approached the ground at an incredible velocity, hurling wheels of fire." The text also speaks of a ray that could incinerate entire armies and provoke, among the survivors, the falling of fingernails and hair, as well as describing the weapon of Agneya: "An arrow that had the dazzling splendor of smokeless fire was launched. ... The world, burned by the heat of that weapon, seemed gripped by a fever. Even the waters became hot, and the creatures that lived in the waters seemed to burn. The enemies fell like trees burned by a devastating fire." The descriptions cannot fail to recall the tragedy of Hiroshima and Nagasaki. What happened at Mohenjo-daro thousands of years ago and why today it still seems radioactive is a yet unsolved mystery.

THE PILLAR
OF ASHOKA
India

*In the heart of most spiritual India,
a colossal iron pillar has challenged the rains
without ever rusting for over 1500 years.
How is this possible?*

In New Delhi, the sprawling metropolitan capital of India, we find one of the greatest enigmas of the past: a mysterious iron column, also known as the Ashokan pillar. Not everyone among the thousands of tourists who crowd the Quwwat-ul-Islam complex every year knows the importance of the manmade object found in the courtyard of the ancient mosque.

The mosque and the gigantic 74 m (243 ft) minaret were built in the 12th century during the Muslim domination of India. The iron pillar of Delhi, however, is a "standard of Vishnu" at least 1600 years old, an object of worship that must have been part of a Hindu temple, not a mosque.

We do not know where it came from, or who produced it, and above all, we do not know how an iron pillar could have resisted 16 centuries out in the open without having been destroyed by rust.

Made of solid iron, the column is over 7 m (23 ft) tall and weighs nearly 7 tonnes: the pillar must have been made of wrought iron. How it could have been possible to create a work like this without modern technology remains an unsolved riddle. The most impressive part of the column is the capital: the eight pieces that compose it were designed, forged, and assembled with absolute precision. On the

269 BC - Ashoka of the Maurya dynasty becomes emperor of India.

232 BC - Emperor Ashoka dies.

c. AD 400 - Chandragupta II, emperor of the Gupta kingdom, has the first inscription carved on the pillar of Ashoka.

2010 - Laboratory analysis of the iron pillar leads to the supposition that it was produced and originally placed in Udayagiri, in eastern India.

top, there is also a rectangular hole that probably housed a circular disk of metal, a chakra. Among the different significances of the chakra, one was that of a weapon of the god Vishnu: a deadly, tapered disk. Vishnu hurled the chakra, and when the disk reached his enemies, it decapitated them before returning into his hands like a boomerang.

Laboratory analyses conducted in 2010 demonstrated that the pillar's exceptional resistance to corrosion is due to a thin film of oxide and the high phosphorus content of the iron. The secret, according to scientists, is the type of iron that was used. But 1600 years ago, who could have been capable of producing a substance of this sort? In the Madhya Pradesh, a region in central India, there was an ancient tribe, the Agaria, who by tradition had always extracted and worked the iron. Their secret consisted in selecting a particular type of iron ore that did not rust because it was rich in phosphorus.

One of the major puzzles concerning the pillar of iron was where it was originally located. An inscription on the monument affirms that the column was erected at *Vishnu-padagiri*, a hill with a footprint of Vishnu. And in the zone of Vidisha, in Madhya Pradesh, one can find a hill with a very unusual form: seen from above, it shows, in fact, the outline of a gigantic footprint. The hill of Udayagiri is located along the line of the Tropic of Cancer, an ideal site for astronomical observers, who flourished in this very zone. The incredible column of Delhi might thus be what remains of a very ancient, forgotten observatory. And its shadow would have aided ancient priests in understanding the sky above them. A plausible hypothesis, at least until the precious metal disk, now lost, that once adorned it is found again.

MOGUI CHENG
China

The "City of Demons" seems to take on a sinister life during the nights of the inhospitable Chinese desert.

In the Chinese autonomous province of Xinjiang, we can find the lowest point (in the Taklamakan Desert, 155 m or 509 ft below sea level) as well as the highest point (the peak of K2, with its 8611 m or 28, 251 ft) in the People's Republic of China. Also in Xinjiang, we find the point of land most distant from any sea on the entire planet: this point in the Dzoosotoyn Elisen Desert is 2648 km (1645.4 mi) from the closest seashore. It is a region of the world where nature appears extreme and at times unwelcoming. It is a meeting place for the stories and legends of many different peoples all bordering together: Mongolia, Russia, Kazakhstan, Kyrgyzstan, Tajikistan, Afghanistan, Pakistan and India. The famous Silk Road passes through this area, and there is still a vivid suggestion of the echoes of ancient armies crossing it, recounted by Marco Polo or by whoever recounted the exploits of Genghis Khan. Legend has it that one of these armies disappeared into nothingness, swallowed up by a demonic song and a sinister sandy wind. It happened in the Urho District, 100 km (60 mi) north of the city of Karamay, in the unsettling ghost town of Mogui Cheng. They also call it "the Nuomin Wind (or Ghost) City," while the Mongols refer to it as Sulumuhak, "the Castle of Specters."

Mogui Cheng is not really a city; it is an amazing desert area covering

53 BC - A Roman legion disappears in the Chinese desert.

c. 1218 - Genghis Khan conquers the Mogui Cheng region.

c. 1273 - The Venetian merchant Marco Polo crosses the Xinjiang desert.

1884 - The Qing Dynasty in China founds the province of Xinjiang, which means 'New Frontier'.

30 sq km (11.6 sq mi), where gusts of wind and tumultuous rain have eroded and shaped the terrain, resulting in imposing and disturbing structures that actually recall the abandoned ancient castles, towers, and dwellings of a ghostly city. But there are also human and nonhuman faces, terrifying profiles of unknown demons, as were masterfully immortalized in the film *Crouching Tiger, Hidden Dragon*, the 2001 Oscar-winner.

Here the wind blows relentlessly 24 hours a day, reaching speeds difficult to find recorded on dry land, but which can be found on the open sea, such as winds of storm force 10. By night, sands fly, stones bump together, and terrifying sounds chase one another around the curves of the structures of the "ghost town."

According to local tradition, these would be the voices of demons that torment Mogui Cheng, or the diabolical ranks of Yen-lo-wang, the Taoist divinity known as guardian and judge of hell.

In stepping through the crackling pebbles of Mogui Cheng, those who are more fortunate find gems of red carnelian, also known as the "crystal of the oracle," owing to its presumed magical properties allowing seers to look into the past. And for this city, the past means a boundless loneliness and desolation, but also an entirely different story: that of lakes where dinosaurs came to drink hundreds of millions of years ago, to the south of Dinosaur Valley, before the great cataclysm that swept them away forever. But this is truly another history, one that also transited through the valleys and peaks of this enigmatic and fascinating region of China.

THE PYRAMID
OF XI'AN
China

The largest tomb in the world was to contain everything conquered in life by Qin Shi Huang, the man who unified China.

At 2 km (1.2 mi) from the city of Xi'an, in the Chinese province of Shaanxi, exists an extraordinary world: hundreds of mounds of earth that rise among the farms, some of medium size, others gigantic. What is contained inside them is still a mystery, but we know who was buried there: emperors, generals, nobles, some of whom were the richest and most powerful persons ever to live on earth.

Some 2000 years ago, these lands were the theater of bloody wars; massive armies clashed and dynasties rose and fell. All around echoed the sounds of thousands of workers engaged in building tombs. Monuments of a fantasy world, which was to continue even after death: symbols of power and wealth, status symbols that were to last for eternity.

The most important of these tombs is also connected to the most powerful of curses. In 246 BC, a united China still did not exist. A series of small kingdoms fought among one another for supremacy. In the region of Qin, a very young sovereign, who had just inherited the throne, ordered the construction of his own tomb. The tombs of important people were supposed to be built upon higher ground, and that

221 BC - Qin Shin Huang unifies the various kingdoms of China under his rule.

210 BC - Qin Shin Huang dies and is buried in his monumental mausoleum in Xi'an.

1974 - Some farmers discover the terra cotta 'Army of Xi'an'.

1987 - Emperor Qin Shin Huang's mausoleum is placed on the UNESCO World Heritage List.

2008 - Twenty of the soldiers in the terra cotta army are exhibited in the British Museum, London.

of the king was supposed to be the highest of all, so the builders chose a site on the slopes of Mount Li. What they could not have known at that point was that the mausoleum they were building was to become one of the greatest works ever created on earth. The child-king of Qin succeeded in later years in unifying the kingdoms into a single empire under his command: thus was born the empire of Qin, or China.

The architects were now called upon to create a monument for the most powerful man in all of Chinese history: an entire royal palace, reproduced underground, in the interior of a mountain created for the occasion. An artificial mountain that measures about 350 m (1150 ft) per side and 70 m (230 ft) in height. It was realized using over 3.5 million tonnes of earth, carefully pressed. It was much more than a tomb; it covered nearly 6000 ha (23 sq mi) of terrain and constituted one of the largest funerary complexes ever built in the world.

Ancient accounts describe the burial place in these terms: "On the ceiling shone the heavenly constellations. The floor reconstituted the realm of the Emperor, with rivers and oceans made of mercury and replicas of all his royal palaces, ready to welcome his soul. The entirety was surrounded by everything he would need for governing in the beyond, just as he had done in life." The grave goods must have been impressive. One need only think that there was not even any mention of the entire army of 8000 terra cotta soldiers, the spectacular "Army of Xi'an" that was interred near the tomb.

The entire world of the Emperor was replicated by forging bronze and terra-cotta, but also by offering blood tributes. Beyond the hundreds of propitiatory human sacrifices, in fact, the lives of thousands of workers were consumed: they worked from dawn until sunset, until the exhaustion of their energy, deprived of food and sleep, until death. All the Emperor's citizens had to spend one year of their life in service of the construction of the tomb. Many, however, remained there much longer and never returned home.

Then there is another question: according to historical records, at the end of the building process, the tomb supposedly measured 150 m (492 ft) in height, much higher than it is today. A pyramid of that height would have to have a base of 500 m (1640 ft) per side, that is, five times greater than its current size and four times larger than the Egyptian pyramids. Experts believe that the reduced dimensions we see today are owing to the prolonged action of winds and rains, which have eroded the enormous mound of earth. But another theory suggests that the tomb is lower because it was never completed. In 210 BC, when the Emperor died, the people rebelled against the atrocities they had endured and put an end to his dynasty forever. Perhaps Qin's mad dream to re-create an underground empire, so that he could be accompanied in the afterlife, failed. But what remains alive instead, after more than 2000 years, is the most incredible of his undertakings: the unification of China. A nation traveling full kilter toward a leading role in the near future.

THE RUINS OF YONAGUNI

Japan

An incredible underwater fortress seems to have sunk off the coast of Okinawa. They call it "the Sea Palace."

In the ocean abysses of the westernmost point of all of Japan, the archipelago of Ryukyu, lies an ancient mystery. Off the shore of the small island of Yonaguni, underwater explorer Kikachiro Aratake made a sensational discovery in 1985: a majestic rock formation, a sort of underwater pyramid, shaped and sculpted, apparently by human hands. The exceptional discovery immediately raised questions about the dating of the unusual structure, as well as the identity of the unknown builders who thousands of years ago erected this temple forgotten on the sea floor.

After years of research coordinated by Masaaki Kimura, professor of oceanography at the University of Ryukyu, the data regarding the incredible underwater discovery seem to identify a single block of carved stone, 20 m (66 ft) high, 200 m (656 ft) deep, and 100 m (328 ft) wide. The structure is pyramidal, with huge terraces, stairways, and genuine avenues within it.

Some geologists maintain that the structure could only be the work of nature, a combination of natural underwater events that could have brought about a spectacular and geometric erosion of the submerged pyramid. According to Professor Kimura, however, there are two possible scenarios, which correspond to two

1985 - The underwater explorer Kikachiro Aratake discovers the rock formation of Yonaguni.

1997 - The Japanese industrialist Yasuo Watanabe sponsors research on the Yonaguni structure.

1998 - A violent underwater earthquake strikes the island of Yonaguni.

2007 - Masaaki Kimura, professor at the University of Okinawa, dates the Yonaguni structure to 2000-3000 years ago.

possible datings. In the first scenario, the entire area would have been submerged by the melting of glaciers from the last glaciation, with the consequent rising of sea levels, some 10,000 years ago. According to this hypothesis, a very ancient, unknown civilization would have been annihilated during the climatic upheaval. In the second scenario, the archaeological complex of Yonaguni would date back to a more recent epoch: between 4000 BC and 400 BC. In this case, it would have ended up at the bottom of the sea as a result of one of the devastating earthquakes and tsunamis that cyclically affect this region of the planet.

Many inhabitants of the island cite an ancient local legend that tells of the exploits of Taro Urashima, the hero who was borne on the back of a turtle to "the underwater palace of the god of the sea." This is the very animal that appears to be sculpted within the Yonaguni structure. One section of the pyramid, in fact, is called the "Sacred Area" owing to certain curious discoveries found inside it: a bird of stone, a triangular basin, and a block sculpted in the form of a turtle, very similar to the *kamekobaka*, the turtle-shell tombs typical of the Okinawa tradition.

Around the central body of Yonaguni, a terraced structure, runs a circular route between 6 m (20 ft) and 50 m (164 ft) wide, bordered by a low wall that opens only at an arched gate. Outside this ring, which defines the perimeter of the principal pyramid, five other, smaller edifices rise.

The façade of the construction is oriented toward the south, and it is from here that the stairs begin that lead to the two areas called the "Sacred Area" (to the east) and the "Terrace" (to the west), the latter being characterized by suggestive rock sections perpendicular to one another and perfectly cut at right angles.

At the highest level of the structure are three large cylindrical holes that can accommodate large pillars, which perhaps collapsed, and a trap door leading to a room below, inside which a dolmen is housed. Another structure, called *Goshintai*, contains a fascinating stone that, according to certain researchers, could have functioned as an ancient sundial.

Outside the main complex, the other buildings are all connected by walkways, such as the one leading to the fascinating megalith similar to one of the Moai on Easter Island. It is 7 m (23 ft) high, and at its upper part, has some engravings that seem to suggest facial features; there are two horizontal fissures called "the eyes of Jacques," in honor of the deceased Jacques Mayol, the great French diver who was enamored of the pyramid of Yonaguni.

Could the enigmatic underwater structure of Yonaguni be the work of nature? Or must we rather think of a civilization that disappeared thousands of years ago without leaving any other traces of itself besides this underwater pyramid? Among the supporters of the human hypothesis, there are many who call into question the legend of Mu, the hypothetical continent that supposedly existed in the distant and forgotten past, before disappearing right into the Pacific between Japan and South America.

The only thing certain is that, for the dates indicated by scientists as possible periods for the realization of the underwater structures of Yonaguni, no known evolved civilization inhabited the Japanese island. The truth about the Yonaguni pyramid seems to be well-guarded on the ocean floor.

ANGKOR

Cambodia

*In the heart of Cambodia, forgotten for
centuries in the forest, an ancient and
wonderful secret is sculpted in stone.*

Angkor, in Cambodia, is an impressive place, shrouded in mystery. An ancient city, today it is considered one of the great marvels of our planet. Angkor Wat is the most famous temple and its name derives from the ancient Sanskrit; in the Khmer language, it means "the temple of the capital." It is a magical place, with extremely suggestive architecture: it is not by chance that it has become Cambodia's major attraction or that an image of it now appears on the Asian country's national flag. But within it, many yet unresolved mysteries are concealed. The walls of the sacred temples of Angkor, in fact, enclose a very ancient history: its stones and its bas-reliefs recount an incredible legend, suspended between sky, stars, and prophecies.

Viewed from above, the entire Angkor Wat complex appears like a map. Its principal building is an *equinoctial structure*, that is, oriented according to the east-west axis, and arranged in such a manner that at the spring equinox, the sun rises over its central tower. Then, the number 72 plays an important role: apparently the ancient builders wanted to emphasize this number in a very obvious way within the architectural complex. Perhaps it is only a coincidence, but there are also 72 architectural structures of Angkor

c. 1150 - The Khmer king Suryavarman II orders construction of the Angkor Wat temple.

13th century - The Chinese explorer Daguan Zhou claims that the Angkor Wat temple was built in only night by a divine architect.

1586 - The Portuguese Antonio de Madalena is one of the first Europeans to visit the monument.

1860 - The French naturalist and explorer Henri Mouhot visits Angkor and executes the first famous illustrations of the site.

Wat, and 72 is the number at degrees of longitude that separate it from the legendary Pyramid of Cheops to the west, and 144 (72 x 2), the number of degrees from the Moai of the Easter Island to the east.

And nothing at Angkor Wat seems to have been left to chance. We need only think that there are four epochs of Hindu mythology – the Krita Yuga (which lasts 1,728,000 years), the Treta Yuga (1,296,000 years), the Davpara Yuga (864,000 years), and the Kali Yuga (432,000 years) – and the sections at Angkor register exactly the same values if measured in *hat* (the local unit of measure, equal to about half a meter). Whoever built this architectural jewel knew exactly what the numbers of this place were supposed to represent.

If we were to think about a link between the great mythical places of our planet, this could probably be represented by the stars. This fantastical hypothesis has sparked some of the most incredible theories: the design of the buildings of Angkor, for example, would appear to reproduce the constellation of Draco, in the same manner in which the Pyramids of Giza appear to reproduce the belt of Orion. Draco the Dragon, however, was visible during the spring equinox at the latitudes of Angkor for the last time in 10,500 BC. This was the same era when the Sphinx of Giza was reflected on the horizon with the constellation of Leo, which the Sphinx would represent, according to certain views. It is a fanciful theory that would overturn everything we know about the history of ancient civilizations of our planet. As far as we know, 12,000 years ago there were no civilizations well enough developed to be able to produce works of this magnitude and complexity.

Official archaeology, however, establishes that the construction of Angkor Wat took place between the years 1113 and 1150, by order of Suryavarman II.

But among the 1200 sq m (12,917 sq ft) of spectacular and detailed bas-relief carvings that adorn the buildings of Angkor Wat, there exists an interesting clue: sculpted in the stone is a tale from Hindu mythology called the "churning of the ocean of milk." According to some, this would be a metaphor describing a specific scientific theory: the precession of the equinoxes, a fundamental astronomical phenomenon for those observing the skies.

In the relief, the Asura (gods) and the Deva (angels) pull on the coils of the serpent –which would represent the constellation of Draco – wrapped about Mount Mandara, to facilitate the transition from one astrological age to the next. And thus explaining why the sky we observe changes slowly through the centuries.

One final curiosity: in the temple of Ta Prohm, one of the few temples have not been restored, another curious engraving ignites tourists' fantasies: the "dinosaur bas-relief." It's an animal figure that bears a strong resemblance to the prehistoric stegosaurus, a creature that became extinct 140 million years ago, when humans did not yet live on this planet.

ULURU
Australia

*The pulsating and mysterious heart of Australia is
an enormous rock, at the center of the Australian
continent's arid desert and of the ancient
knowledge of the Aborigines.*

Australia is one of the most ancient lands on the planet. It is as mysterious as it is rich in resources, a continent that in some periods of the year becomes arid and inhospitable. Here, in this huge land, more than 50,000 years ago, what is perhaps the most ancient civilization still existing on our planet arrived: men and women who appear to have had mysterious sensory abilities, knowledge now lost for the rest of the world.

The center of Australia – also called its "red heart" on account of the color of its earth – is an arid place, hiding secrets that have not yet been revealed, beginning with the unusual geological forms of certain sites. The most famous is the legendary site of Uluru, but the same enigmas also cross through Mount Conner, with its flat top, and Kata Tjuta, a marvelous place that is sacred for the Anangu.

The English Captain James Cook was the first European to explore the coast of Australia in 1770. At that time, the Aborigines were estimated to number between 300,000 and 1 million. They divided into many tribes or clans, each of which spoke a different language; there were more than 500.

Many scientists have long studied the shamanic

1873 - The Australian explorer William Gosse sights the Uluru rock and names it Ayers Rock in honor of the governor of South Australia, Henry Ayers.

1936 - The first tourists visit the Uluru site.

1950 - Uluru is declared an Australian national park.

1985 - The Australian government gives the property of Uluru back to the Pitjantjatjara (Anangu) Aborigines.

1993 - The Australian government establishes the English-Aborigine name of Uluru/Ayers Rock for the site.

powers of the Aborigines: the first anthropologists who visited the Australian tribes told of having seen men who had extraordinary powers, such as being able to climb up a rope suspended in the void, to fly, to appear or disappear at will, to levitate, to see through bodies, to traverse long distances in an instant, as well as telepathic communication and clairvoyance. Many sacred Australian places are forbidden to those who are not Aborigines, because the energy of these sites is considered to be so powerful as to overwhelm those who are not capable of enduring it.

The culture of the Aboriginal people is the oldest in the world, older even than the Assyrian-Babylonians or the Egyptians. But how long have the Aborigines lived in Australia? The most ancient archaeological sites date back to about 40,000 years ago. One of the most important Aborigine areas is that of the Northern Territories, a region as large as Italy, France, and Spain put together. Here a major part has been found of the testimony of the millennial presence of the Aborigines.

At 460 km (286 mi) from Alice Springs, the city standing at the center of the continent of Australia, we find one of the most mysterious places in the world: its name in the Aborigine language is Uluru; the English call it Ayers Rock. It is the largest monolith on our planet, the most ancient rock in Australia. Its perimeter is 10 km (6 mi) and it rises 348 m (1142 ft) high: a colossus that is continually changing its color, through the entire range of red, in accordance with the hour of the day and the season. The most exciting moment, however, is doubtlessly twilight, when Uluru shines of its own accord, monumental and magical amid the dark desert surrounding it.

The Aborigines consider it to be the principle of the creation of the world, linked to ancient legends of what they call "the dream time." Uluru is a sacred site, powerful, charged with energy. Here they still celebrate shamanic rites. Some caves still conserve sacred paintings narrating the very ancient history of the earth, which the Aborigines consider to be a dream materialized.

In the Aboriginal view of the world, time is not linear: words do not exist for *past* or *future*. The memory of the fathers, passed down exclusively by word of mouth for thousands of years, recounts the stories of "the dream time," when the first beings emerged from the earth, from the sky and from the sea, taking on the forms of living beings and moving about the territory, giving life, with their bodies, to men, plants, and animals. Although known by many names, today they are commonly referred to as Ancestor Spirits.

Uluru is an important place for the Aborigines because many ancestors passed through here and their traces would still be visible today. They are part of the territory and form part of the dense network of sacred sites, connected to one another by the pathways called "songlines." Some scholars believe these are lines of particular geomagnetic force that the Aborigines can perceive owing to their particular sensitivity and expertise. Certainly, people followed some of these pathways during migrations – just as birds do in flight – that are vital in such an inhospitable land.

By contrast, geology considers the bizarre rock forms that can be seen everywhere as the simple result of the erosive action of atmospheric agents. But also as the result of a meteorite shower that 4700 years ago devastated this area of the planet. In any case, a force from heaven.

Area 51
United States

The most controversial military base in American history seems to conceal top-secret military activities, fueling the most extreme of science-fiction theories.

Each day from the Las Vegas airport, airplanes take off that belong to an airline company called "Janet." The company does not exist but is indirectly owned by the U.S. Air Force. Each airplane transports more than 100 persons to a top-secret location in the Nevada desert. A military base on which thousands of military personnel are working in strict confidentiality on inconceivable projects. They call it Area 51, and for over 60 years it has been a mystery with which journalists, historians, ufologists, and conspiracy theorists have been testing themselves.

Extending for 26,000 sq km (10,038 sq mi), the area is entirely militarized and under strict surveillance. In order to reach its borders, you need to take the special exit off State Highway 375, the one that the state of Nevada has officially rechristened "Extraterrestrial Highway," a name that refers directly to legends involving this military base and the numerous sightings of unidentified flying objects reported by motorists traveling along it.

The entire area is wedged between the desert, the skyline of the mountains, which seem to want to protect it from prying eyes, and the dry bed of the salt flat Groom Lake: they call it Dreamland. Inside the

1947 - The so-called Roswell incident takes place in New Mexico: the remains of a supposed alien spaceship that crashed are said to have been taken to Area 51.

1955 - The CIA chooses Area 51 as a secret place to test the Lockheed U-2 spy airplane.

1962 - Area 51 also used to develop the OXCART project for the construction of military reconnaissance aircraft.

1977 - F-117s are tested in Area 51.

2013 - For the first time the CIA publicly acknowledges the existence of Area 51.

area one can make out dozens of hangars, the most famous of which is Hangar 18: a structure about 100 m (328 ft) in width and length, and over 30 m (98.4 ft) high. One wonders what sort of aircraft a structure of such dimensions is designed to contain. Thanks, again, to satellite imagery (the airspace, in fact, is strictly off-limits, even to pilots of the nearby Nellis Air Force Base) we can make out the very long runways, huge strips of asphalt in the middle of the desert. Some exceed 3 km (1.9 mi) and the longest reaches 7 km (4.3 mi), an unusual size for a common landing.

But what you can see from above is only a small part compared to what appears to be hidden from curious eyes. Witnesses speak of a structure extending underground for more than 50 stories, with increasingly restricted levels of access, and of mile-long tunnels branching off all throughout the underground.

The extremely high levels of secrecy surrounding Area 51 – just consider that for decades the U.S. government has denied the very existence of the base – have given rise to all sorts of assumptions about what is happening inside: from top-secret technology projects to military tests to the presence of traces of extraterrestrials.

All the hypotheses revolve around the words of people who claim – without having incontrovertible evidence, however – to have entered within the confines of Area 51. Among these, the most famous is doubtlessly Bob Lazar, a self-styled physicist who claims to have worked near the base and seen tests of spaceships made out of nonterrestrial materials.

But the most incredible legend is the one known under the name of the "Roswell Incident." On 2 July 1947, a mysterious object fell from the sky at Roswell, New Mexico. The remains were rapidly hidden away by the military, and the incident was shrouded in secrecy. Although government sources deny the event, ufologists believe that what fell at Roswell was a spaceship with extraterrestrial pilots inside. Many believe that the mechanical components of the vehicle and the biological remains of the aliens were brought directly to Area 51. Supposedly an autopsy was performed on the aliens, similar to the one represented in the famous Santilli film, which the English producer himself admitted to having falsified. But Santilli also swore that he had been inspired by an original film that he had seen with his own eyes.

Beyond the science-fictional theories, it is within the confines of area 51 – patrolled by Jeeps armed with assault rifles, monitored by latest-generation radar, under surveillance by military helicopters flying over, and surrounded by motion sensors hidden on the ground – that the American government has supposedly tested some of its most incredible prototypes over the course of the years.

In 1955, the Lockheed Corporation, in agreement with the CIA, chose the area to test the legendary U2 spy plane, constructing the first nucleus of what would later become the legendary Area 51. Then came the CIA's Project Oxcart: ultrafast aircraft for high altitude reconnaissance, from the first Blackbirds of the 1960s, to the F-117s of the 1980s, on to the latest top-secret prototypes for drones and aircraft supposedly capable of reaching extremely high speeds, such as Mach 6, or of making an entire circuit around the planet in less than five hours. The truth about Area 51 lies under the sun in the Nevada desert, but still remains invisible to the eye.

THE SAILING STONES

United States

In the California desert of Death Valley, heavy stones move about for no apparent reason, leaving behind mysterious tracks in the soil.

D eath Valley, in California, is an infernal desert. This lowest point in America has been measured at its center, where the highest temperature of the continent, 56.7°C (134.1 F°), was recorded. Something unexplainable occurs at Death Valley, a phenomenon that agitates those who come upon it and challenges scientists. In the area called Racetrack Playa, boulders, even the enormous ones, move by themselves through the desert, leaving a mysterious track on the ground. The phenomenon is known as the *sailing stones.*

The rocks, which come primarily from a nearby dolomite hill, move several meters (yards) every two or three years, leaving different trails, which are very straight if the stone has a rough surface, but more erratic if the surfaces of the rock are well polished. Sometimes one single trail presents two distinct types of paths, a sign that the mass has suddenly been overturned during its mysterious shifting. Other times the trajectories veer abruptly, forming surprising angles. The depth of the trails never exceeds 3 cm (1.2 in).

Scholars seek to understand how these rocks, abandoned in the desert, some weighing hundreds

1915 - Joseph Crook offers the first testimony of the 'sailing stones' phenomenon in the Racetrack Playa site.

1948 - Geologists Jim McAllister and Allen Agnew make the first mapping of the Racetrack Playa area.

1972 - Bob Sharp and Dwight Carey monitor the movement of 30 stones, identifying them by name.

2014 - The results of experiments and research are published, stating that the combined action of the wind and ice is responsible for the movement of the 'sailing stones'.

of pounds, can move without any apparent force. Is it a natural phenomenon, or in the heart of Death Valley is there a yet unknown force that causes them to move?

Racetrack is a perfect name for what goes on at Racetrack Playa. It is the bed of an exceptionally scenic dry lake, extending more than 4 km (2.5 mi) in length and 2 km (1.2 mi) in width, at an elevation below sea level. Its surface is incredibly flat; there is a difference in elevation of only 4 cm between the northern edge and the southern.

The history of the sailing stones began in 1948 when geologists McAllister and Agnew began systematically mapping the area. *Life* magazine produced an unforgettable photo shoot on the topic. In 1972, 30 of the boulders that had moved during that year were identified, and each one of these was assigned a name so as to follow its shifts throughout the following seven years. The results were interesting: no rock ever moved during the summer; they only moved during the winter (even though in some winters there was no movement). The longest single itinerary was registered for a rock named Nancy, which traced a groove of 201 m (660 ft). Karen, the heaviest, with its 318 kg (700 lbs.), by contrast, never moved during the seven years of the test.

Possible explanations of the phenomenon all point to the role of ice, which freezes a part of Death Valley during the winter. Various experiments were performed in laboratories of several universities, but not all were fully convincing.

The latest occurred in 2011 and were confirmed in 2014, and the results were published in the prestigious *American Journal of Physics*. According to the scientists, the phenomena could be explained by a combination of light winds and small formations of ice called "rafts." Yet even the most satisfactory scientific explanation fails to minimize the emotion of encountering a rock that, during the night, in the inhospitable Death Valley, has embarked upon a journey with no apparent destination, even though its solemn advancement has left a visible trace for the telling. For some, this would be a surprising metaphor of our own existence.

THE DISAPPEARANCE OF THE ANASAZI

United States

*What happened to the ancient Indian people
who lived in the suggestive
Chaco Canyon of New Mexico?*

Pueblo Bonito is considered the greatest archaeological mystery of the United States. About 800 years ago in the New Mexico desert, an entire tribe consisting of over 8000 persons suddenly disappeared, leaving a series of traces, all to be deciphered. This population was known as the Anasazi, *the People of the Eagle*, and their name in the Navajo language signifies "the Ancient Ones."

Chaco Canyon in New Mexico is 19 km (11.8 mi) long and 1500 m (0.9 mi) wide, and it is here that the Anasazi people lived peacefully before disappearing.

It all began in the late 18th century when, almost by chance, some explorers arrived at Chaco Canyon. At the base of the canyon, they found an imposing construction consisting of 800 dwellings: Pueblo Bonito, the home of the Anasazi. Some think this was their capital, while others believe it was a spiritual center. One thing certain is that at the time of its construction, sometime around the year 1000, nothing of the sort existed in this arid zone of North America. It was an absolutely pharaonic complex for the epoch. Round, underground and circular, the kivas are the compound's most famous architectural element. The largest of this kind is the *Casa Rinconada*, just outside Bonito, 20 m

c. 1140 - The Anasazi people abandon the Chaco Canyon site.

1823 - The governor of New Mexico, José Antonio Vizcarra, makes the first exploration of Chaco Canyon.

1901 - Richard Wetherill carries out research at Pueblo Bonito.

1907 - United States President Theodore Roosevelt proclaims Chaco Canyon a "national monument".

1987 - Chaco Canyon is placed on the UNESCO World Heritage List.

(65.6 ft) wide and 5 m (16.4 ft) high. The kivas were probably used for sacred ceremonies: they were constructed with holes in their roofs through which spirits could enter or exit, according to the liturgy of the vanished ancient tribes.

The Anasazi had a devotional relationship with nature, especially with the Earth and the Sun. In many kivas, the ray of sunlight coming through the windows at dawn at the summer solstice went to strike a specific niche found within the construction. This phenomenon has yet to be interpreted, but it becomes even more obvious at the site of *Fajada* Butte: the rock engraving of the "sun dagger" represents two spirals; owing to the formation of the cracks in the rocks at the entrance to the cave, the larger spiral is crossed by a veritable blade of light at the summer solstice. At the winter solstice, however, the sun penetrates into two cracks delimiting the outer borders of the spiral. It is a sort of calendar from a very ancient era engraved in stone.

In addition to being oriented in accordance with the surprising astronomic knowledge of the Anasazi, the kivas themselves were also built upon precise points on the ground. These sites, chosen by the shamans, manifested what they interpreted as a strong Earth-energy, represented by a spiral.

Another obsession for the Anasazi people was represented by their network of major roadways. They constructed over 300 km (186 mi) of roads, a majestic example of which is the Great Road of the North overlooking Pueblo Bonito: 33 km (20.5 mi), traced out with an astonishing precision. It would be difficult to realize such an alignment even with a compass, an instrument the Anasazi did not possess. This demonstrates that their knowledge was much more advanced than what traditional archaeology is capable of imagining.

But there exists another disturbing aspect of this culture. Scientific studies conducted on human remains found in Chaco Canyon appear to demonstrate that the Anasazi were a people dedicated to cannibalism. There are numerous indications: fractured skulls, bones drained of their marrow, organic proofs in the fossil excrement, and even traces of myoglobin (a protein found in muscle) found among the deposits in a pot. Also present in the midst of this desert is a significant tomb, that of Richard Wetherill, one of the first explorers to arrive in Chaco Canyon. He was murdered by the very people he wanted to study.

His testimony, however, is significant. Wetherill writes: "When we entered Navajo Canyon and discovered the ruins, we went back into our own world an unknown number of centuries. Everything was intact, exactly as it had been left by the original inhabitants. The objects were arranged in the rooms as though the persons had just left to make a visit to their neighbors. Perfect examples of crockery were lying on the ground, while iron utensils and other household items had been left in the places where the Anasazi women had used them for the last time."

A striking scene, the one described by Wetherill: an advanced civilization forced suddenly to abandon its center, with no signs of battle or epidemics. The mysterious destiny of the Anasazi, the tribe of the Ancient Ones, remains an enigma.

THE BERMUDA TRIANGLE

Atlantic Ocean

*One of the planet's greatest mysteries,
a sea afflicted by an incredible series of naval
and air calamities.*

A stretch of the Atlantic Ocean is known as the sinister theater of one of the most famous legends in the world: that of the curse of the Bermuda Triangle. An unsettling portion of sea, bordered by Puerto Rico to the south, Florida to the west and the Bermuda archipelago to the north. Enormous ships, entire air squadrons, and above all, hundreds of human lives, have literally disappeared – without apparent cause – into these waters.

The unexplainable events that appear to occur cyclically in this triangle of ocean date back to ancient times. Already at the time of the pirates, ancient mariners cursed the pitfalls of what they called the Sargasso Sea, populated by mysterious ghost ships and troubled by difficult navigation. But there is one day on which the legend of the Bermuda Triangle was truly born: on 5 December, 1945, a beautifully sunny day, the entire Squadron 19 of the U.S. Air Force mysteriously disappeared. Five military aircraft, with five officers and nine soldiers aboard, were participating in a simple exercise not far off the coast of Florida. Suddenly they began sending confused messages to the control tower: they indicated that they were lost, their words were confused, and the instruments of all the planes were out of order. There was no further news from them.

1492 - Cristopher Columbus notes strange behavior on the part of the compass while navigating in the Bermuda Triangle.

1918 - The American warship *USS Cyclops* disappears.

1945 - U.S. Air Force Squadron 19 takes off from Florida and vanishes, leaving no traces.

1950 - Edward Van Winkle Jones writes an article for the Associated Press with the data regarding the inexplicable Bermuda Triangle incidents.

To bring relief to the squadron, a Martin Mariner even took off from the coast, a hydroplane with a crew of 13. This also disappeared into nothingness. In the days following the mysterious event, not even more than 4000 hours of flight resulted in finding a single wreck of one of the six airplanes that disappeared into the sea. All this is even more disturbing if we think about the fact that the squadron planes were capable of landing gently in the sea and staying afloat for 90 seconds, while their crews were trained to leave the aircraft in 60 seconds, and they even had life rafts available.

But the tragic list of airplanes that vanished into thin air in the Bermuda triangle is very long. Even if we consider only the most sensational disappearances, we come up with this bewildering list: in 1947, a Skymaster C-54 airplane of the U.S. Army disappeared with six soldiers on board; in 1948, a four-engine Tudor IV with 31 persons on board; also in 1948, a DC-3 with 32 passengers; in 1952, a British York Transport with a crew of 33; in 1954, a U.S. Navy Super Constellation with 42 seamen on board; in 1963, two Boeing KC-135s; in 1965, a C-119 with 10 passengers; in 1972, an Eastern Airlines flight with more than 100 victims.

But even merchant ships and military ships, genuine giants of the sea, have disappeared into the Bermuda Triangle without a trace. In this case as well, the list is only partial: in 1800, the *USS Insurgent* with 340 passengers aboard; in 1814, the *USS Wasp* with a crew of 140; in 1880, the British frigate *Atalanta* with 290 men on board; in 1918, the *Cyclops* with 306 persons on board; in 1931, the *Stavenger* and her 43 men; in 1938, the *Anglo-Australian* with 39 men; in 1951, the battleship *Sao Paulo* with eight men; in 1963, the *Marine Sulphur Queen* with 39 persons; and in 1973, the *Anita* with 32 men aboard.

Moreover, even in Christopher Columbus's ship's log, strange phenomena were indicated as having occurred in this area, especially during the historic crossing of 1492.

On Thursday, 13 September, 1492, the Genoese navigator wrote: "On this day, at nightfall, the compass needles moved to northwest, and in the morning, they moved rather toward the northeast (...)."

Two days later, the diary pages reported: "As night was falling, they saw a marvelous streak of fire falling from the sky, at four or five leagues from the ships." And on Monday, 17 September, 1492: "The pilots took stock of the situation and acknowledged that the compasses did not indicate the proper direction; and the seamen were fearful and distraught, though they did not say about what."

Many hypotheses have been advanced to explain the mystery of the Bermuda Triangle: from water spouts to seiche waves; from alien abductions to lethal CAT (clear air turbulence). The most recent scientific theory, however, calls methane hydrate into question: colossal gas bubbles that periodically detach from the bottom and would be capable of swallowing up entire ships and setting low-flying airplanes afire.

CHICHÉN ITZÁ

Mexico

Between apocalyptic prophecy and enchanting architecture, the most resplendent heart of the Maya Empire has yet to reveal the last of its secrets.

While Europe was living in the Dark Ages, the Maya civilization was flourishing on the Yucatán Peninsula of Mexico: immense cities were built in the middle of the tropical forest, rich with marvelous pyramids and magnificent temples. There is one location, however, which, more than others, links religion with astronomy. Chichén Itzá, rising upon an area of 3 sq km (1.2 sq mi), was one of the most important Maya cities. The site includes many buildings, each different and incredibly fascinating. The most mysterious, however, are the legendary pyramids of Kukulkán, the El Caracol astronomical observatory, and the famous Pelota ball court, besides, obviously, the Cenote of Sacrifices, to which an entire chapter of this book is dedicated.

Caracol means spiral staircase and refers to the interior stairway of the ancient astronomical observatory.

Its entrances are aligned with the vernal equinox, while other elements recall astronomical events regarding the moon and the legend of the Serpent God, the bringer of knowledge. During the day, the Maya studied the movements of the sun, analyzing shadows cast inside the building, while at night, they observed the reflections of the stars within the great stone receptacles filled with water. The Maya

c. 750 - Chichén Itzá becomes regional Maya capital.

c. 1200 - Beginning of a period of decline for Chichén Itzá.

1843 - The American explorer John Lloyd Stephens carries out the first exploration of the site.

1972 - The site, at first private property, is now run by the Mexican federal government.

2007 - Chichén Itzá is voted one of the New Seven Wonders of the World.

were profound observers of the night sky; they knew the movements of the universe, the stars, and the planets, and in this manner established their legendary calendar. Their scientific knowledge was based on religious beliefs. The Maya appeared to be aware that our galaxy, the Milky Way, is a spiral, and that a black hole can be found at its center. In fact, for the Maya, the god of creation was Hunab Ku, represented in the form of a spiral from the center of which it created life by means of powerful explosions. For some, this would be a clear religious metaphor describing the Milky Way.

The principal monument of Chichén Itzá is a marvelous pyramid, which also is closely connected to astronomy: Kukulkán, according to myth, was the Serpent God from whom the Maya obtained their knowledge and whose return they awaited. The pyramid dedicated to the god is constructed in such a manner that, on the day of the equinox, the sun illuminates the northwest stairway, creating a shadow that appears just like an enormous serpent. Moreover, the pyramid was built so that on 21 December, 2012, the well-known date concluding the cycle of the threefold Maya calendar, the northwestern edge would project a play of lights on the steps. This covered with the head of the serpent sculpted at the base of the stairway, illuminating it. For some, this is the sign of the return of the Serpent God.

But at Chichén Itzá, there is also an imposing playing field designed for playing the game of Pelota: 170 m (558 ft) long and 50 m (164 ft) wide, it is surrounded by perimeter walls reaching nearly 8 m (26 ft) in height. Pelota was a very violent game, but it was greatly loved by the Maya, a sacred game.

The aim of the game was to cause the ball to pass through a ring of stone fixed at about 7 m (23 ft) above ground: the first team that managed to score was the winner. A macabre panel in the central courtyard of Chichén Itzá, however, depicts the beheading of a Pelota player; some argue that this was the fate of the defeated. A more recent interpretation maintains instead that it was the captain of the winning team who was to be decapitated. The glory consisted in the honor of being sacrificed to the gods: a victory that led to death, a way to be considered on the level of a god. But there are also some who believe that the entire game of Pelota was nothing more than an elaborate metaphor for representing the astronomical phenomenon of the procession of the equinoxes: extremely important information for someone who was obsessed with the movements of the stars and with calendars.

There remains the mystery of how it could have been possible for the Maya to gain such highly developed astronomical and architectural knowledge, and, above all, from whom did they learn it? The depressing response is reported in the diaries of John Lloyd Stephens, the explorer who in 1841 told of his discovery of Chichén Itzá: "We were sitting on the edge of the wall and we tried in vain to penetrate the mystery surrounding us. Who were the people who had built these cities? When one finds oneself among the ruins of the Egyptian cities, or even in those of Petra, the foreigner knows the history of the persons to whom those ruins belonged. But when we asked the Indians about it, their monotonous response was always the same: *quien sabe?, who knows?*"

THE MAGIC
OF THE CENOTES
Mexico

*The most unattainable treasure chest
of the Maya is hidden under water, in an
incredible network of underground tunnels.*

All the most flourishing civilizations of antiquity developed around great rivers: the Nile for the Egyptians, the Euphrates for the Babylonians and the Indus for the Harappan civilization. For the Maya, however, there were no rivers. The Yucatán is a peninsula with no mountains and no surface watercourses. The terrain is calcareous and porous, so that any water that falls becomes rapidly swallowed into the depths of the earth, creating freshwater wells and abundant underground sources, which, however, would have been inaccessible if a meteorite had not fallen some 65 million years ago into the Caribbean Sea, ripping open, with an apocalyptic rain of rocks, the surface of the earth in a jagged series of points. Those points are what today we call the cenotes, enormous natural wells. For the Maya, the cenotes represented the possibility of survival in an otherwise inhospitable land, and for this reason they were considered sacred. The cenotes provided for life, and through them one could enter into contact with the ancient gods who, according to the Maya, lived in the underwater depths of Mother Earth.

Today it is estimated that on the Yucatán Peninsula alone exist some 30,000 cenotes: some of

1904 - Edward Thompson explores the cenotes at Chichén Itzá in search of precious ancient finds.

1926 - The Mexican government accuses Edward Thompson of having illegally taken finds from the cenotes to the United States.

1944 - The Mexican Supreme Court absolves Thompson, 9 years after the explorer's death.

2010 - Researchers find the most ancient human remains on the American continent in the water of the Hoyo Negro cenotes.

them are easily accessible, others are reserved for archaeologists, while still others are unexplored. Many of them
connect to one another by an amazing network of underground caves, channels, and lakes, some of which are majestic. Stalactites and stalagmites unite to form spires or entire
welded columns, making these underground environments
seem like underwater cathedrals.

The Maya had strong ties with these caves, and they celebrated important ceremonies in their sacred waters. The first
reports in this regard are from the diaries of Bishop Diego
de Landa. If he was responsible, on the one hand, for the
destruction of the writings of the Maya, causing the cancel-
lation of a major part of history that we might have known,
on the other hand, he did leave us an account of what he
observed directly: the bloody Maya rituals. For the Maya,
physical pain was one of the means by which it was possible to make contact with the divine: for this reason, they
inflicted upon themselves terrible injuries and, after having
fallen into a trance, threw themselves into the cenotes, ready
to communicate with the gods. Also into the cenotes they
threw priceless treasures as well as young children and babies
to be drowned in sacrifice.

On the basis of these stories, in 1904, American explorer
Edward Herbert Thompson decided to set off in search of
the underwater treasures of the Maya. He searched among
the ruins of Chichén Itzá, one of the most representative
centers of the Maya Empire. Its name means "on the edge
of the well of the Itza." Thompson found the two cenotes
of Chichén Itzá and decided to dive in, making use of a
rudimentary diving suit, a tube for breathing, and weights

tied to his shoes. In the attempt, he almost lost his hearing, but at over 40 m (131 ft) deep, he found everything that was told by the legends: precious treasures and fearsome skeletons, including those of children. Thompson discovered what would be called the "Sacred Cenote" or the "Cenote of Sacrifice." Not far away, he identified another cenote, called Xtoloc, which was used for the population's water supply. The Cenote of Sacrifice measures 60 m (197 ft) in diameter and is over 80 m (262 ft) deep, but in order to access it, you need to make a dive from the ground of about 20 m (66 ft). Beside the cenote stands an ancient building, probably utilized for purification ceremonies for the sacrificial victims. Today, more than a century after Thompson's first daring dive, the cenotes still represent a challenge even for the most experienced divers. The network of caves and galleries connecting them spreads over at least 133 km (83 mi): an entire underground region, and mostly unknown. These inaccessible caverns still conceal many treasures. Bones and offerings have been conserved here for many centuries, discouraging even the most daring plunderers. The cenotes are veritable "time capsules" that have remained intact. Soon, perhaps, using technologies still inconceivable to us, we shall succeed in deciphering them. And they may reveal to us the secrets of the Maya people and their knowledge that was lost in the blaze along with their manuscripts.

UXMAL
Mexico

*One of the jewels of the Yucatán contains
its incredible history within its name,
meaning "built three times."*

Uxmal is an ancient city of the classical period of the Maya civilization, a UNESCO World Heritage Site. It is located in Mexico, about 80 km (50 mi) from the sea, in a hilly region of the Yucatán. It is characterized by a particular architectural style called Puuc, marked by rich tiles decorated with sacred figures, which cover the rough stone, and rich ornaments of exquisitely carved stone reliefs.

In the Maya language, the word *uxmal* means "built three times." The area was inhabited in ancient times, but the actual city was founded only in the 7th century AD, by the Xiuh family, which continued on until the 10th century, when it was occupied by the Toltecs. As throughout the Yucatán, water resources were scarce, and for this reason the most highly venerated of all the divinities was Chac, the god of rain. In 1200, the city was completely abandoned – possibly owing to the malevolence of Chac – and the jungle soon swallowed it up. Not before the passing of seven centuries did Uxmal see the light again in the 19th century.

The area extends over 1 km (0.6 mi) north to south and over 500 m (0.3 mi) east to west. Inside are eight groups of sacred buildings and buildings of power: the Adivino

c. 500 – Foundation of the city of Uxmal.

c. 1200 - Uxmal begins to decline and is gradually abandoned.

1838 - The French explorer Jean-Frédéric Waldeck publishes the first detailed description of the ruins of Uxmal.

1921 - In an article, Stansbury Hagar claims there is a correspondence between the Maya sites and the constellations.

1996 - Uxmal is placed on the UNESCO World Heritage List.

(Pyramid of the Magician), the Nunnery Quadrangle, the Governor's Palace (with a marvelous throne in the form of a two-headed jaguar), the House of the Turtles, the Pelota ball court, the House of the Witch, the Cemetery Group, the Temple of the Phallus, and the House of the Pigeons.

In front of the governor's palace is a broken monolith, a sort of cylinder with a conical tip that has provoked much discussion: there are some who consider it to be a tribute to fertility and others who hypothesize that it is a mysterious object that came from the sky and drove itself into the ground.

However, the most imposing and suggestive building is doubtlessly the Adivino (also known as the Pyramid of the Dwarf or of the Magician), which dominates the area with its 35 m (115 ft) of height. What make it so unique are its rounded edges (a characteristic found only here) and its elliptical base. On its summit stands a temple entirely decorated with ominous masks, which would represent the jaws of the powerful god Chac. According to local legend, the entire edifice was constructed in one single night by a dwarf with the aid of his mother's magical practices. Probably it was the temple of an oracular divinity that manifested through a priest-prophet. The virtual line joining the pyramid with the center of the Nunnery Quadrangle marks the point on the horizon where the sun sets on the day that it passes through its zenith.

According to Stansbury Hagar, an ethnographer who wrote in the first half of the 20th century, the skulls and bones decorating the façade suggest that the temple is dedicated to the god of death. The wide access road toward the western façade, according to the scholar, forms an open mouth: the jaws of a human face. It is the symbolic depiction of the death one must pass through in order to enter into contact with the magician who issues the prophecy. The pyramid also represents the constellation Scorpio, which is connected with the god of death. Stansbury Hagar performed extensive research on Uxmal, and in 1921 he published a paper on the correspondences between the zodiac and the temples there. His hypothesis is that all the cities sacred to the Maya were designed to reproduce a celestial pattern. This is because the Maya believed that the microcosm corresponded to the macrocosm, and that everything on earth was an imitation or reflection of the perfect reality existing in the universe. The sacred city that imitated the heavenly vault would thus attract to itself a portion of that perfection.

In studying the positions and iconographic characteristics of the individual architectural elements found on the map of Uxmal, Hagar succeeded in identifying each one of these as referring to one of the 12 constellations of the zodiac, on the basis of correspondences he found (except in the case of Aquarius, for which nothing more than a small collapsed temple remained). Moreover, it is certain that the Maya had astounding levels of knowledge regarding the sky and time, as is demonstrated by their complex and very precise calendars, and their ability to predict eclipses. How they could have developed their knowledge, however, and how much of their prophecy is true, remains to be discovered.

TEOTIHUACÁN
Mexico

The city where the gods are born.
One of Mexico's greatest mysteries.
Who built it? And why was it abandoned?

For many centuries, Teotihuacán has been the largest metropolis of Central America, the heart of a civilization that dominated ancient Mexico for over 500 years. It was the cradle of a civilization, and even today it is wrapped in mystery. It has, however, left us an immense treasure: hundreds of surprising artifacts and masterpieces that recount the history and culture of one of the most fascinating peoples of pre-Columbian America.

Founded 200 years before Christ, Teotihuacán today is still the vastest archaeological site of Central America.

A broad boulevard, 2.5 km (1.6 mi) long, crosses the city, dominated by two imposing pyramids: the Pyramids of the Moon and of the Sun. The latter, with a perimeter of 900 m (2953 ft) and a height of 71 m (233 ft), is the third largest pyramid in the world. But after years of study and archaeological investigations, many questions remain unanswered: What people founded this great city?

What was their story? And why did they suddenly abandon their city?

Temples, pyramids, statues, masks: the legacy of Teotihuacán is carved in stone, but no written document has come down to us. It is hard to believe that such an

c. 200 BC - Foundation of the city of Teotihuacán.

5th century AD - The apogee of Teotihuacán.

7th century AD - Beginning of the decline of Teotihuacán.

1905 - The Mexican archaeologist Leopoldo Batres carries out the first scientific digs on the site.

1910 - The Pyramid of the Sun is restored on the occasion of the 100th anniversary of Mexican independence.

1987 - Teotihuacán is placed on the UNESCO World Heritage List.

advanced civilization could be unacquainted with writing – unless someone had wanted their memory to be canceled forever. What is most striking about Teotihuacán is its city plan: 22 sq km (8.5 sq mi) of streets rich with buildings.

The architects of Teotihuacán knew highly advanced constructional techniques, such as the one referred to as *talud-tablero*, which consisted of alternating a horizontal platform (the *tablero*) with an inclined wall (the *talud*). This architectural style, first used here, was later employed by the Maya and by many other peoples of Central America in building their own pyramids. And yet no subsequent civilization was able to build a structure as imposing as those of Teotihuacán.

Among their most incredible edifices, beside the two great pyramids dedicated to the sun and the moon, there is the Temple of the Feathered Serpent. It is a smaller pyramid, but rich with bas-reliefs and impressive decorations. As an example, the finely sculpted head of the serpent could weigh as much as one tonne. And originally, the temple had more than 360.

Teotihuacán was a very important spiritual center: many of the divinities worshipped here continued to be venerated by many other peoples until the arrival of the Spanish conquistadores. The capital of a genuine empire, Teotihuacán was a cosmopolitan city as well as being situated at the center of important commercial routes. Its culture profoundly influenced all the peoples of Central America, including the Maya and the Aztecs. It was long believed that the people of Teotihuacán were pacific, but more recent excavations have brought to light murals and statues of warriors.

Furthermore, just like in many pre-Columbian cities, in Teotihuacán as well, bloody rituals were practiced, including human sacrifices.

In recent years, archaeologists have found, at the bases of the Pyramids of the Sun and of the Feathered Serpent, some skeletons of decapitated humans, with the hands bound behind the back. An impressive image, to be added to the various depictions of bleeding hearts pierced by large daggers. And these very daggers are still intact: elaborated in disturbing forms with sharp black obsidian, they were used during sacrificial ceremonies.

During its period of greatest expansion, Teotihuacán had about 200,000 people who lived in more than 1000 residential complexes.

Still visible are the large architectural structures and the immense artistic treasures, including mural pictures, decorated ceramics, statues, and hypnotic masks. The human faces are represented in a stylized manner, with precise geometric proportions and inscrutable expressions. Theirs is a highly symbolic art that transmits great composure and solemnity.

Teotihuacán reached the peak of its splendor around the 5th century AD, but it was entirely abandoned just two centuries later. The reasons for its decline remain a mystery. Just as the origins of this incredible city, and of the people that built and governed it without leaving any written testimony, remain mysterious. And lastly: what was the true name of that which the Aztecs called "the city of the gods"? What gods actually lived there?

THE OLMECS
Mexico

*Huge stone faces that seem to reveal an ancient
history, one that has never been told.*

T hrough centuries of domination and occupation of the Mesoamerica region, the Spanish conquistadores never heard of them. They knew the Incas, the Aztecs, the Maya, without understanding all their secrets, but they never imagined that all these peoples descended from one single mysterious civilization: the legendary Olmecs, an enigmatic people and very powerful, forgotten for entire generations.

The term Olmec derives from the Nahuatl language spoken by the Aztecs and means "rubber people," referring to the many rubber trees within their territories. The Olmec civilization seems to have developed around 1200 BC, principally in three large centers of Mexico: San Lorenzo Tenochtitlán, La Venta, and Tres Zapotes. But their influence went well beyond these boundaries and embraced entire areas in Guatemala, Belize, El Salvador, Honduras, Nicaragua, and Costa Rica.

An ancient Maya poem narrates how the Olmecs arrived from a land of rain and fog "in a certain era/ that no one can calculate/ that no one can remember." Why they then sud-

c. 1200 BC - The Olmec civilization flourishes.

c. 900 BC - The Olmec site of La Venta becomes the principal city of the region.

c. 400 BC - The Olmec civilization begins to decline.

1862 - Mexican antiques dealer José Melgar y Serrano discovers the first colossal Olmec head.

1920 - Archaeologists Frans Blom and Oliver La Farge rediscover the Olmec site of La Venta.

1932 - The mysterious low relief known as El Rey at Chalcatzingo is discovered.

1938 - American archaeologist Matthew Stirling begins excavation of the Olmec site of Tres Zapotes.

denly disappeared around 400 BC remains an unsolved mystery.

The discovery of the Olmecs is owed primarily to archaeologist Matthew Stirling. While on a mission for the Smithsonian Institution, he succeeded in bringing to light the remains of this incredible vanished civilization, and in dating it as preceding all the other civilizations known at that time.

The most famous discovery is doubtlessly that of the enormous stone faces that, since that time, have become the very icon of the forgotten Olmec people: 17 colossal sculpted heads, distributed among the sites at San Lorenzo, La Venta, and Tres Zapotes. What raises doubts and fantasies about these exciting works in basalt is the set of facial features represented: they are not Amerindian. Rather, they have Asiatic characteristics (at San Lorenzo) or African ones (at La Venta). Certain Olmec engravings on steles, moreover, seem even to portray European features. It is difficult to believe that these would be errors owing to imprecisions of the ancient artists, seeing that in their other sculptural representations, the Olmec demonstrated almost an obsession for anatomical details of perfectly represented men and animals. And on the other hand, it is difficult to conceive that this is simply fortuitous, that characteristics of men actually existing on this planet were reproduced accidentally, even while they were completely unknown to the ancient inhabitants of Mesoamerica, at least according to the history we know.

Throughout the eight centuries during which the Olmec culture developed, although their history is still largely unknown, certain concepts were elaborated that left a mark on all successive cultures.

A people that apparently vanished suddenly perhaps held the knowledge that opened to the Maya the secrets of the heavens and of the calendar. The Olmecs, by contrast with peoples who were their contemporaries, seemed to live in the future and to know objects such as the wheel, the lens and the astrolabe.

The fanciful hypotheses based on these clues have found their confirmation in the bas-relief called *El Rey*, "the king," discovered at Chalcatzingo, an Olmec archaeological site. Carved directly into the mountain wall, the bas-relief represents a curious scene that lends itself to different interpretations. The one verging most nearly on science fiction identifies the carved glyphs as clouds, falling rain, and at the center, a large "ship" sailing through the air, leaving a prodigious wake. Driving it is the king, who holds in his hands an object similar to a gear lever. A sort of photograph "snapped" into the stone, of an event that was unforgettable in the eyes of the sculptor.

The only thing that is certain is that around 400 BC, the Olmecs disappeared suddenly: their cities were destroyed and their imposing statues were knocked down, decapitated, buried. And with them, all the ancient secrets of the most mysterious people of all of Latin America disappeared as well.

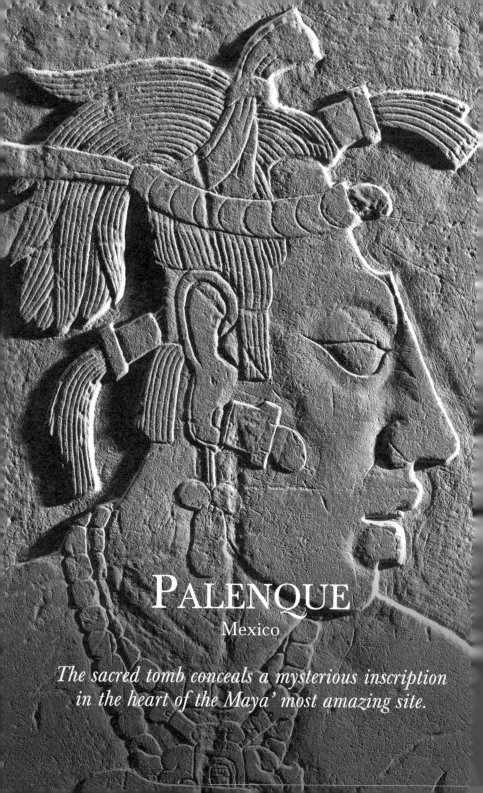

PALENQUE
Mexico

*The sacred tomb conceals a mysterious inscription
in the heart of the Maya' most amazing site.*

Chiapas is one of the poorest states in Mexico, but it is rich with incredible and mysterious archaeological wonders. One of its major attractions is certainly Palenque, one of the main sites of the Maya civilization. The friar Pedro Lorenzo de la Nada discovered it in 1567, christening it Palenque ("the Fortress"). The most important buildings of the site are the Temple of Inscriptions, the Palace, and the Group of Crosses. The ruins extend over an area of about 3 sq km (1.2 sq mi): according to many, however, this would represent only 10 percent of the original surface, and a good part of the city would still be concealed in the forest.

The palace is an architectural complex connected by a network of courtyards, rising at the center of the archaeological zone. The Group of Crosses is an ensemble of pyramidal temples with bas-reliefs relating the principal events of the local mythology.

The Temple of Inscriptions is a grand funereal monument dedicated to the legendary King Pacal. The name of the temple refers to the incredible hieroglyphic inscription that it bears: the second longest in all the Maya cities. The

c. 220 BC - The Maya city of Palenque is founded.

AD 683 - The king of Paleque, Pacal the Great, dies.

8th century – The city of Palenque begins to decline.

1567 - Friar Pedro Lorenzo de la Nada is the first European to visit the ruins of Palenque.

1840 - John Lloyd Stephens and Frederick Catherwood visit Palenque and create marvelous illustrations of the site.

1952 - The Mexican archaeologist Alberto Ruz Lhuillier discovers the tomb of Pacal the Great inside the Temple of Inscriptions.

building is a pyramid of rectangular base nearly 30 m (98.4 ft) in height, at the top of which an 11 m (36 ft) high temple stands. Some of the stones with which it was built even reach weights of 15 tonnes and are positioned at its top. But it is at the foundation that its most precious treasure was found. While he was examining the temple floor in 1952, Mexican archaeologist Alberto Ruz Lhuillier managed to move the stone that was covering an unexpected secret passage. A long marvelous stairway opened out before his feet: it led to the legendary tomb of King Pacal, the one that would later be defined as "the most important tomb of the entire Mesoamerican zone." Here the archaeologists discovered a precious colossal sculpted sarcophagus, rich with ornaments and bas-reliefs.

The find that most sparked the fantasies of researchers is the stone that covered King Pacal's sarcophagus, the one that has become famous as "the astronaut's stone." On the slab is a depiction of a man who, according to supporters of theories verging on science-fiction, appears to be driving an aircraft with rocket propulsion. The figure appears to have in his fist a sort of gear lever, and at the rear of the presumed aircraft, an engine is identified, from which emanate tongues of fire.

There are also some who have identified a pilot's seat in the bas-relief, as well as a mask for breathing, and in general, an aerodynamic fuselage.

In a famous and highly criticized book from 1968, Erich von Daniken affirms that the sarcophagus stone is definitive proof of the presence of an alien civilization in ancient Mexico. Obviously the scientific community rebelled at this, labeling such texts as ludicrous. Archaeologists believe, rather, that the depictions represent a priest – or perhaps King Pacal himself, who died in 683 AD – captured at the moment of passage between terrestrial life and the beyond: the man was thus not embarking upon interstellar space travel but, more simply, experiencing death. Even if perhaps the two events were, after all, not so distant in the eyes of the Maya, a people extremely attentive to the movements of the heavens and the perfection of their constellations, which they must have studied and replicated on earth. Perhaps realizing eternal masterpieces, such as the marvelous and enigmatic Palenque.

Las Bolas

Costa Rica

*Mysterious and perfect stone spheres appear
in different places on the planet.
But their native land is Costa Rica.*

Costa Rica is a small country in Central America: 4 million inhabitants who welcome 1 million tourists every year. Most visitors are attracted by the idyllic nature of the country but others come in search of what is considered to be an incredible unresolved enigma: *Las Bolas*, the mysterious stone spheres of Costa Rica.

The story began in 1930 when excavators came across spheres of stone with an impressive frequency, which they were unable to explain: they were too perfect to be manmade, and too incomprehensible to be the work of nature. The spheres were discovered in various areas, but especially along the course of the River Diquis, with an astonishing concentration in the locality of Palmar Sur. The smallest spheres have a diameter of 1.5 m (4.9 ft), while the largest are over 2 m (6.5 ft); they are all of granite and can weigh more than 20 t. In addition to their nature, the site of their discovery raises many questions: the closest granite quarry, in fact, is 50 km (31 mi) away from the river delta. Who could have been capable of transporting spheres of such dimensions over rough and uneven terrain? One of the problems encountered in attempting to understand the spheres is that they are timeless: it is not possible to date

1930 - While felling trees, United Fruit Company laborers find the first giant stone spheres.

1948 - American archaeologist Samuel Lothrop directs the first in-depth study of the Costa Rican stone spheres.

1998 - Ivan Zapp publishes a study that connects the spheres to an old wide-ranging navigational map.

2014 - The sites in Costa Rica with the mysterious stone spheres are placed on the UNESCO World Heritage List.

them, they have no inscriptions, they are not connected to any known civilization, and it is not possible to intuit their function. And yet there are hundreds of them strewn all around the country. Some scholars, by means of indirect dating of deposits, maintain that they have established that the spheres date back 2000 years. But the technique by which they could have been produced remains unimaginable in view of the level of perfection shown by the artifacts: the spheres are perfectly polished and they reproduce the elementary geometric solid precisely.

Other scholars maintain that the original arrangement – altered through the course of the centuries, especially for the lighter spheres, which today adorn many roads and dwellings of various towns and villages – might have reproduced heavenly constellations. Probably they would be all that remains of a mysteriously vanished civilization preceding the Maya by several thousand years.

Considering the absence of firm scientific references, the field of hypothesis has become populated with fantastical theories: the most famous is the one formulated by Estonian scholar Ivan Zapp, who, in reference to the work of American archaeologist Samuel Lothrop, related the spheres found at Uvita, on the Pacific coast, to the homonymous island in the Atlantic Ocean. According to this interpretation, the line uniting the two places named Uvita would cross through a village by the name of Bolas and the gigantic Cerro Chirripò, dominating Costa Rica from its height of 3820 m (12,533 ft). The spheres would thus constitute the points on a navigational map even though they would only be visible from above.

Regarding Chirripò, one of the trails climbing the mountain is called "the trail of the burial place of the Golden Machine" by locals. Its name recalls the popular belief according to which a legendary flying object was buried at the top of the mountain. The reflections of light from the perfectly polished *bolas* would have constituted an incredible aerial map for this flying "object." Impossible theories have been advanced, but none seems to satisfy all the questions. All we know is that they are extremely old. And that their secret seems to resist the flow of time unscathed as well as their granite does.

El Dorado
Brazil

The hunt for the most fabulous treasures of South America, hidden in the Amazon forest, is never over.

The name of El Dorado indicates a lost city, covered in gold. According to legend, it was a world created by the gods to conserve our planet's most ancient knowledge. One wonders whether there is any truth to this myth. Was El Dorado only a dream? Or did this enchanted place truly exist somewhere? Various people have searched for the legendary lost city of gold.

Among these, Percy Fawcett, the British colonel who penetrated into the most unknown territories of the earth, and was probably the inspiration for the film character of Indiana Jones, dedicated his very life to the myth of El Dorado. In 1901, Fawcett was charged by the Royal Geographic Society to draw up maps of South America. In the course of his research, he became aware of a legendary manuscript; among its pages, the road to El Dorado seemed to be concealed.

The legend of El Dorado was born in the 16th century, when King Charles V decided to send legions of treasure-hunting explorers into the

1536 - The Spaniard Gonzalo Jimenes de Quesada heads an expedition into unexplored areas in Peru in search of El Dorado.

1537 - The *conquistador* Sebastian de Belalcazar leads his army through the mountains of Ecuador in search of fabulous treasures.

1753 - A Portuguese soldier describes, in the so-called Manuscript 512, his visit to a city hidden in the Brazilian rain forest.

1925 - The English explorer Percy Fawcett disappears in the Brazilian jungle during an expedition in search of the mysterious city "Z", identified with El Dorado.

2001 - The Italian Mario Polia finds, in the Compagnia di Gesù archives in Rome, a document that supposedly proves the existence of the city of El Dorado.

South American colonies. In 1536, Gonzalo Jimenes de Quesada and Sebastian de Belalcazar reported the story of a native chief who took pleasure in covering himself with gold before diving into a lagoon. More than 100 official expeditions were organized in an attempt to identify the elusive city of El Dorado, situating it first in Florida, then in Venezuela, but also between Peru and Bolivia, and lastly, in Brazil in the Amazon forest region. Even Hitler supposedly organized secret research expeditions in Amazonia.

In 2001, the Italian anthropologist Mario Polia discovered an extraordinary manuscript in the Jesuit archives in Rome: it tells of a legendary lost city, hidden by a waterfall, inside the Amazon rain forest. In this document dating from 1600, the Jesuit father Andrea Lopez writes about having found the city and requests that the pope be personally notified.

Another document, equally old and fascinating, is conserved at the national library in Rio de Janeiro. Known as "Manuscript 512," it is the diary of a Portuguese soldier dating from 1753: it relates that during a scouting mission, while entering the forest from the Brazilian side, he came upon an incredibly gorgeous city surrounded by jungle. In particular, he describes a circular plaza housing a large statue of black basalt, pointing north. And all around, there were astronomical symbols and depictions of the planets of the solar system.

In 1920, Percy Fawcett had in his hands not only Manuscript 512, but also a basalt statuette which he identified as the miniature of the statue described in the manuscript. Upon the statuette were engraved 22 letters of an unknown alphabet; these same symbols recurred in the manuscript. For Fawcett, this was proof of the existence of El Dorado. Fawcett organized two large expeditions in the Amazon region: in the Mato Grosso and in the Northeast. But the Mato Grosso is an impenetrable and boundless region, and it is extremely difficult to discover its secrets. Fawcett sought the support of the indigenous tribes, living with them, gaining their trust and overcoming trials of initiation. Eventually, he managed to obtain the information that El Dorado was to be found in the Serra do Roncador, an immense, unexplored area between the Rivers Xingù and Araguaia. For the Indians, this zone was populated by strange presences: a sacred place, not to be desecrated. Today is a military area, forbidden to the public: we know only of the *Gruta dos pezinhos* ("the cave of the little feet"), an archaeological site dating back thousands of years, where one can admire curious footprints of beings with two, three, four and six toes.

Fawcett was convinced that he would succeed in finding El Dorado, in spite of the fact that the Indians had advised him not to venture into the Serra do Roncador: the explorer's last letter, dated 29 May, 1925, was addressed to his wife, Nina: "We are here, at Dead Horse Camp, the exact point where my horse died in 1920 [...]. I hope to be able to resume travel very quickly and finally reach the much-discussed waterfall [...] I am well. I compensate for my advancing years with an unwavering enthusiasm [...] you must never fear I shall fail."

Nothing more was ever heard about Fawcett and his expedition companions, and their fate remains a mystery. Some believe they were killed by the savage inhabitants of the Serra do Roncador, while others prefer instead to imagine that the explorers actually found El Dorado. And that they are still there, waiting for the rest of the world to join them.

LINEAS Y GEOGLIFOS DE NASCA

PAMPA DE SAN JOSE

THE NAZCA LINES

Peru

For whose eyes were these colossal designs
traced in the arid Peruvian desert?
Who could and should have seen them
from such a great height?

I n the middle of the Peruvian desert, which covers about 300 sq km (116 sq mi), the famous Pan-American highway runs, unique in the world, for 27,000 km (16,750 mi). But this zone is also important for other reasons, much more ancient than the famous *carretera*. Dozens of airplanes fly over this area to admire an incredible archaeological site, designated in 1994 as a UNESCO World Heritage Site.

Discovered in 1926 by Peruvian archaeologist Julio Tello, the mysterious Nazca Lines became famous thanks to American geographer Paul Kosok, who flew over the area in 1939 in a small airplane. From the ground, one cannot recognize anything other than a series of small shallow furrows in the soil. From a height of 14 m (a tower has been built on the site for tourists) the reading improves, but only slightly. Only in flight can one clearly see the more than 200 designs and over 13,000 geometric figures that inexplicably fresco the Peruvian desert. The geoglyphs are of cyclopean dimensions: from a minimum of 25 m (82 ft) to a maximum of 275 m (902 ft).

It is not possible to give a certain dating for this highly extravagant manmade work. It is presumed to be very ancient and thought that only the particular arid climate of the region has prevented time from canceling it out. Here the sun shines for about 1200 hours each

1926 - The Nazca Lines are first discovered by Peruvian archaeologist Julio Tello's team.

1939 - American scholar Paul Kosok begins to study the Nazca geoglyphs.

1995 - The Nazca Lines are placed on the UNESCO World Heritage List.

1998 - Death of the German scholar Maria Reiche, who dedicated her life to the study and conservation of the Nazca Lines.

year over a highly mineralized surface and creates a thermal vacuum reaching up to 1 m (3.3 ft) in height; for this reason winds, which here are called *paracas*, do not touch the soil.

The legendary Nazca Lines are a sort of bas-relief carved into the ground, to a depth of between 7 and 10 cm (2.8 to 3.9 in). Official archaeology attributes these works to the Nazca, a primitive tribe that supposedly disappeared inexplicably centuries earlier than the appearance of the successive Inca culture. The lines were supposedly traced between 200 BC and 700 AD, utilizing rudimentary means and instruments. How the Nazca could have created such large figures with precision is unclear. And no one even understands what their purpose was.

The most traditional hypotheses maintained that these were sacred paths, utilized during ceremonies connected with the cult of water and fertility of the earth, or indicators of the presence of sources.

According to Paul Kosok, the lines were used as indicators of the dawn and sunset and of other stars. German astronomer Maria Reiche, who spent her life at Nazca, is of the same opinion; she believes that the geoglyphs were used to determine solstices and equinoxes, eclipses of the sun and the moon, and suitable moments for sowing and harvest.

But the question remaining at the heart of the mystery of the Nazca Lines is why they produced designs that can be seen and appreciated only from above. There are some who think about the ancient legends speaking of the *Viracochas*, the mysterious visitors who supposedly brought civilization to these areas: men with light skin, beards and reddish hair, endowed with supernatural powers.

The mysterious mythological figures were able, in fact, the sail the skies.

Beyond the myth, those lines crossing the desert surface leave one truly without words when flying over. The most unusual geoglyphs are those depicting a spider and various types of birds (among them, the condor and the humming-bird) and other animals; moreover, some human figures are represented with strange glowing auras around their heads. Some of the straight lines, all realized with an impressive precision, are more than 8 km (5 mi) long. To increase the sense of mystery, the majority of the animals represented at Nazca are not indigenous to this zone.

The famous Nazca "spider" belongs to a group of arach-nids among the rarest in the world: they live only in the most inaccessible areas of the Amazon forest. The spider is charac-terized by a particular reproductive organ, normally visible only under the microscope. How did the primitive Nazcas come to know about this spider and its unusual reproductive characteristic?

The unsolved mystery of Nazca has fascinated researchers all over the world for decades, evoking science-fiction type theories: according to authors such as Erich von Däniken and Peter Kolosimo, the Nazca figures would be signals and landing strips for extraterrestrial vehicles. Without going to such lengths, we can at least entertain the idea that perhaps what we know about the ancient civilizations of the past is only small part of the truth. The rest seems to have been forgotten – as here at Nazca – under the sands of time.

MACHU PICCHU
Peru

*A jewel set among the inaccessible peaks
of the Andes, an ancient civilization obsessed
by the movements of the stars.*

24 July, 1911: in Peru, a young explorer with a good dose of courage approaches places that until that moment were considered unexplored, discovering, in fact, something important: the lost city of Machu Picchu. The city of a thousand mysteries: Who transported those enormous stones to the top of a mountain so difficult to scale? Who wedged them together so perfectly hundreds, if not thousands, of years ago?

The young explorer was Hiram Bingham, and it was an extraordinary spectacle that presented itself to his eyes. The ruins of Machu Picchu, which in the Quechua language signifies "old peak," are located in a highly inaccessible area of Peru. Perhaps this is why the Spanish conquistadores never discovered it, and why not even the missionaries who settled nearby ever even suspected its existence. According to official archaeology, the area was settled in the 15th century, but according to some scholars, the principal elements of Machu Picchu were oriented in accordance with particular astronomical alignments, from which one could deduce that the original project referred to the period between 4000 and 2000 BC.

The place is enchanting, splendid, especially if appreciated from above

c. 1440 - The Inca emperor Pachacutec conquers Machu Picchu.

1572 - The Inca kingdom in Peru collapses after Tupac Amaru is captured and killed by the Spanish.

1911 - American archaeologist and explorer Hiram Bingham rediscovers the ruins of the Inca city Machu Picchu.

2011 - French researcher Thierry Jamin claims he has found some secret caves in important buildings at Machu Picchu.

while flying. But at the moment of its maximum splendor, it could accommodate only 750 inhabitants. For this reason, some believe it was a place of worship. A curious study performed on the ancient orientation of the plan of the city in relation to the cardinal points would shift its construction to 3172 BC. What is, nonetheless, certain is that whoever did make it up to this remote peak to build a city must have had an important reason for doing so.

In one of the oldest rooms of Machu Picchu, we can recognize two mortars. Some believe they were used to dye clothes, while others think this was actually an astronomical observatory: the tanks filled with water could reflect the movements of the stars so they could be studied. The Incas were the last to inhabit Machu Picchu, but other populations could have lived there before them. The theories on who might have placed the stones at Machu Picchu are numerous. As with the majority of the megalithic ruins found in other parts of the world, some of the constructions at Machu Picchu appear to be veritable "stone computers" for calculating equinoxes and solstices. The Temple of the Two Windows, for example, is clearly an equinoctial construction: the sun was viewed through the two windows of the building.

Even the Temple of the Three Windows was utilized for tracing the movements of the stars and the sun with precision. A staircase carved into the living rock leads to the top of a ridge on which a stone appears like a throne, surmounted by another smaller monolith, called "Intihuatana," the Sunstone.

Being aligned in accordance with the northeast-southeast axis, this also was used for calculating the solstices and equinoxes.

As in other parts of the world, at Machu Picchu we find cyclopean walls realized with dozens of enormous blocks. A puzzle of polygonal stones wedged perfectly together with one another, positioned without any sort of cement. One of the largest is a monolith about 3.5 m (11.5 ft) long and 1.5 m (4.9 ft) wide, with an estimated weight of 200 tonnes.

Another mystery surrounding the construction of Machu Picchu: on the mountain, there was no site large enough to realize the entire complex, so 25,000 tonnes of earth were transported from a valley located 400 m (1300 ft) farther down. And this operation was performed with sheer human force or on mule back to an altitude greater than 2500 m, with its lack of oxygen. Who could have produced such perfect inlays or have cut the stone so precisely, with such expenditure of effort? The Incas themselves indicated that their masters were of a civilization that preceded them, that of the Viracocha. A legendary civilization, venerated by all the Peruvian peoples. What remains to be seen is whether Machu Picchu could have been their most sacred place.

SACSAYHUAMÁN

Peru

An entire city constructed in the form of a puma at the top of the Andes, one of the most sacred sites for the legendary Inca people.

There are certain places that appear, more than others, to be veritable treasure troves of unanswered questions, mysteries dating back to eras that official history does not even contemplate. One such place is certainly the famous ancient Inca capital of Cuzco, Peru. The name of the city, in the ancient Quechua language, signifies "navel of the world." Cuzco is located at 3400 m (11,155 ft) above sea level, and according to official archaeology, the first human settlements would date back to about 3000 years ago. The entire city appears to be built upon a pattern of the outline of a puma, the animal sacred to the Incas as the protector of earthly things.

In his famous volume *Comentarios Reales de los Incas*, one of the earliest accounts of the history of the Incas and the Spanish conquest, Garcilaso de la Vega wrote about the area of Cuzco in 1609: "... constructions of such inconceivable proportions as to suggest that some magic has governed their construction, that they are the work of demons rather than human beings [...] made of stones so large and numerous that one wonders how they got the Indians to produce them, because they did not know iron or steel for cutting and polishing the rock, nor had they oxen or carts to transport them."

1438 - The Inca emperor Pachacutec begins construction of Sacsayhuamán.

1536 - During the siege of Cuzco on the part of the Inca monarch Manco II, the Spanish troops under Pizarro struggle to re-conquer the Sacsayhuamán fortress.

1609 - Garcilaso de la Vega writes the first description of the Sacsayhuamán site.

1983 - Sacsayhuamán and other monuments in Cuzco are placed on the UNESCO World Heritage List.

In the ancient buildings of Cuzco, the stones of green diorite, a mineral that is particularly hard to work, are put in place without any kind of cement. They are worked in such a precise manner that they adhere perfectly to one another: it is not even possible to insert a credit card into the junctures between the stones. It is hard to believe that the Incas, a people who apparently did not possess advanced technology, or even know the wheel, could create such amazing architectural works. And it is even more difficult to imagine how they could have succeeded in shaping the stone as though working with wax, giving it strange forms and developing an ingenious and very sound system of interlocking polygonal blocks. A construction technique that was more refined than those used in Europe during the same period, in spite of the fact that the Old Continent was decidedly more advanced from the cultural, scientific, and technological points of view.

Sacsayhuamán is surely among the most important buildings of Cuzco: a promontory on the outskirts of the city upon which stands an enigmatic construction. The name in Aymara means "place where the hawk is satiated." But if we look at the map of Cuzco as being of the form of a puma, then Sacsayhuamán represents the animal's head, with the zigzag walls recalling the jaws. The entire complex could accommodate tens of thousands of men, and perhaps for this reason the conquistadores called it "the fortress," imagining that it had a military purpose.

Many scholars now believe that instead it was a religious complex, a sacred area, or even one single colossal temple. Legends tell that these walls were already ancient when the Incas settled in these places, but official archaeology rejects this hypothesis, attributing the start of construction, which lasted 70 years, to the Inca emperor Pachacutec in 1438.

At Sacsayhuamán, there are masses as high as 8 m (26 ft), weighing more than 300 tonnes, adhering to one another perfectly in puzzles of different forms. Construction that not even the passing of the millennia has been able to mar. The enigma of the architectural technique used in other buildings at Cuzco – rocks adhering perfectly to one another – develops here on three levels. But the mysteries at Sacsayhuamán do not refer only to the cyclopean walls.

In the area at the top of the monument, what appear to be ancient foundations have been discovered, characterized by plans based on geometric polygons. To date, no definitive answer has been formulated as to the meaning of these enigmatic ruins or on what these foundations are resting. Further, it is hypothesized that the ruins visible today represent only 30 percent of what once stood at Sacsayhuamán: after looting and plundering prolonged over the centuries, in fact, the only thing left at the "fortress" is that which could not be carried away: the stones. The complex is perfectly aligned with the four cardinal points, and the walls intersecting the three circles at its summit have an ideal orientation for determining the winter and summer solstices.

If Sacsayhuamán truly was an ancient astronomical observatory, we must imagine that the Incas were capable of creating a work of such magnitude. Or does it all date back to an ancient past that we still do not know?

LAKE TITICACA
Bolivia and Peru

The geographic heart of one of the oldest civilizations on the planet seems to guard an incredible truth about its untouched depths.

At 3818 m (12,526 ft) elevation, nestled among the Andean peaks on the border between Peru and Bolivia, we find perhaps the most enchanting and mysterious sheet of water in the world: Lake Titicaca. Its hypnotic blue color runs for over 200 km (124 mi) in length and 65 km (40 mi) in width, surrounded by shores of wilderness. It is the world's highest navigable lake and yet in distant times, Lake Titicaca was on the ocean floor. The entire area, in fact, is littered with millions of fossil shells, a sign that the entire plateau was once a seabed, probably thrust upward with the lifting of the earth that formed the entire South American continent. All this would have occurred about 200 million years ago.

Through the course of time, the morphology of the area has undergone other profound changes. In particular, the surface of the lake has undergone significant oscillations, to the point of causing the very bed of the lake to incline, following movements that usually require thousands if not millions of years to unfold. The ancient ruined city of Tiahuanaco, with its colossal docks, must certainly have bordered the water; indeed, recent archaeological discoveries would appear to suggest it may even have been

c. 3100 BC - The waters of Lake Titicaca were about 85 m (279 ft) lower than the present level.

c. 2200 BC - The first human settlements on the Isla del Sol.

1570 - The missionary friar José de Acosta settles along the banks of Lake Titicaca, where he writes his work on the physical features and populations in the New World.

2000 - A team of underwater archaeologists announces the discovery of the ruins of an ancient temple on the bottom of Lake Titicaca.

an island within the lake. But today these ruins are located about 30 km (19 mi) from Lake Titicaca. To be able to explain such an anomaly, we would have to hypothesize some devastating cataclysm that occurred in the area, a catastrophe that would have so drastically lowered the level of the lake, a calamity capable of wiping out any civilization might have lived in the region of Lake Titicaca. A series of apocalyptic events that would very much resemble the description of the myth of Atlantis.

Perhaps it is no coincidence that the famous Andean legend, transcribed by the missionary friar José de Acosta – one of the first Europeans to reach the area – states the following: "For some unnamed crime, the people living in the most ancient times was destroyed by a flood. After that the Creator appeared in human form from the lake and brought back the sun, the moon, and the stars." The Indians spoke of a flood in which nearly all humankind died, and of the god Viracocha who emerged from the waters of Lake Titicaca and brought back life. The story appears, once again, to touch upon the recurring theme of a civilization destroyed by water, just as was the case for the legendary Atlantis. And yet official history contemplates no evolved civilization during the period in which all this would have occurred, namely around 10,000 BC.

There is also something hidden, however, underneath the surface of Lake Titicaca. Some archaeological expeditions conducted at the beginning of the new millennium have identified the underwater ruins of mysterious settlements: the remains of a temple occupying a surface of more than 3000 sq m (0.74 acres), situated 30 m (98 ft) deep. At 70 m (230 ft) depth, moreover, they have identified a road that appears to connect the coast to Isla del Sol. Furthermore, retaining walls are visible 100 m (328 ft) deep, as well as agricultural terracing and much more. The research team also discovered Inca and pre-Inca amphorae, and vases of Amazonian origin. And the fact that the remains have been found at such different depths would appear to be a further confirmation for the hypothesis that the entire zone may have raised and lowered, then inclined to one side. And a flourishing civilization may have existed on the shores of Lake Titicaca much earlier than previously imagined. Perhaps even during the times of the legendary civilization of Atlantis.

TIAHUANACO

Bolivia

*More than a city, it is an immense
and very ancient astronomical calendar
sculpted into the stone, at nearly 4000 m
(13,123 ft) above sea level.*

At 3846 m (12,618 ft) elevation, on top of a barren plateau, nestled between the majesty of the Andes and legendary Lake Titicaca, rises Tiahuanaco: a place shrouded in mystery, one of the most fascinating archaeological sites in the world. Its name means "the city of the gods."

As Pedro Cieza de León reports in his diary in 1549: "The builders of these great foundations and fortifications are unknown, nor do we know how much time has elapsed since their epoch, since today we see only the walls of fine workmanship, erected many centuries ago. Some of these stones are worn and in disrepair, and there are others so imposing that one wonders how human hands could carry them to where they are today. I dare say that these are the oldest antiquities of all of Peru ... I asked the natives if these dated back to the time of the Incas. But the natives, laughing at my question, repeated back to me what I have already said: they were constructed before the reign of the Incas; but they could not indicate or suggest to me who had built them or why."

It is not clear whether Tiahuanaco was the capital of a great empire, but certainly it was a great center of worship where people performed ceremonies and rites of which we know nothing. At the

---

c. 300 AD - Foundation of the city of Tiahuanaco.

c. 1000 - Tiahuanaco is abandoned.

1549 - The Spanish missionary Pedro Cieza de León is the first European to visit the ruins of Tiahuanaco.

1945 - The Austrian archaeologist Arthur Posnansky dates the site to 15,000 BC.

2000 - The ruins of Tiahuanaco are placed on the UNESCO World Heritage List.

peak of their expansion, the city could accommodate about 20,000 people, distributed over more than 2 sq km (0.77 sq mi). This is the largest pre-Inca megalithic architectural work in South America. The history of the mysterious civilization of Tiahuanaco is divided into five periods: traditionally, it begins around 2000 BC and ends – mysteriously – around AD 1200. A civilization about which we know very little: no written texts have been discovered at Tiahuanaco. One certainty is that Lake Titicaca played a central role in the development of the site, and the ruins of the former Tiahuanaco stood right on its shores, as the remains of the area called "Puma Punku" would suggest, probably constituting the point of access to the city from the vanished ancient port. Today, Lake Titicaca is located 18 km (11.2 mi) away, and fully 30 m (98 ft) lower, which causes us to consider the possibility that some cataclysm may have fallen upon this area.

The ruins of the Pyramid of Akapana are situated on a hill reaching 16 m (52.5 ft) in height upon a base 200 sq m (2153 sq ft) wide. Its flat top is the site of a mysterious oval basin. Some believe this had the function of collecting water, while others add that the water was used to study the movements of the planets that were reflected therein. Just to the north rises the Kalasasaya, a platform about 3 m (9.8 ft) high on a base measuring 130 x 120 m (427 x 394 ft), for use in performing unknown rites and ceremonies. One of the impressive aspects of the structure is its method of construction: its extremely heavy blocks of andesite and red sandstone fit together perfectly. Inside stands what is considered to be the very icon of the ancient civilization of Tiahuanaco: the Gate of the Sun.

Fashioned from a single block of volcanic rock, it is finely carved with bas-reliefs and features four mysterious niches. The entire gate has an estimated weight of 44 tonnes; it is the largest elaborated monolith ever discovered on our planet. At the center, the gate is surmounted by an enigmatic anthropomorphic figure that seems to be wielding two scepters shaped like serpents. All around, there are 48 winged figures, of which 32 have human faces and 16 heads of condors. The Gate of the Sun owes its name to the day of the vernal equinox, when the rising sun appears exactly at its center. Many believe the 48 figures and four niches are part of an astronomic calendar sculpted into the stone but not yet deciphered. The entire Kalasasaya, at any rate, does seem like a sort of cyclopean calendar, since major astronomical events illuminate its equinoctial edifices, or monuments connected with the solstices, with the light of the sun.

The true origin of this magical place is still a mystery. According to local legend, it was created by the ancient giants who lived there in primordial times. One of the most incredible theories was formulated by Arthur Posnansky, director of the National Museum of Bolivia and founder of the Bolivian Archeological Society. After a life dedicated to studying Tiahuanaco, Posnansky established that it must have been founded as early as 15,000 BC – in the Ice Age – and that it was later devastated by a cataclysm that proved deadly to its population.

Such fantastical hypotheses even drew Nazi explorers to Bolivia in the 1940s in search of proof of the existence of the legendary civilization of Atlantis. And of what would be the oldest city on the planet.

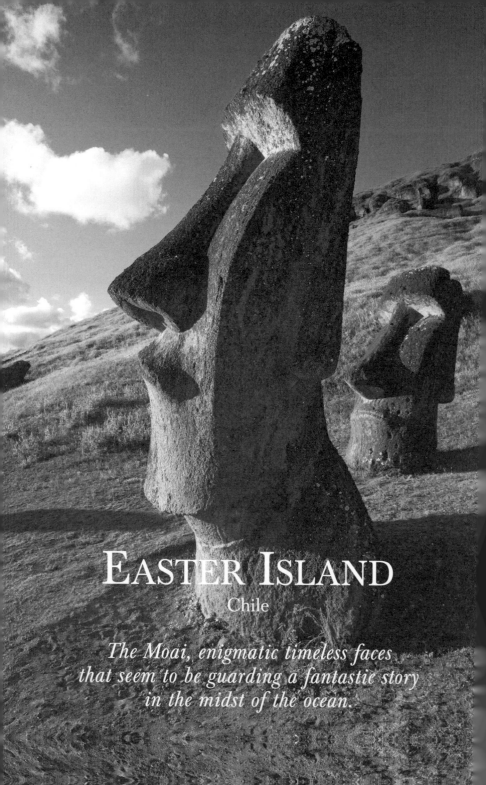

EASTER ISLAND
Chile

*The Moai, enigmatic timeless faces
that seem to be guarding a fantastic story
in the midst of the ocean.*

Rapa Nui, better known as Easter Island, is perhaps the most mysterious island in the world. It is also the inhabited location on our planet most remote from any other inhabited place: nearly 4000 km (2500 mi) of ocean in all directions separate it from any other dry land. If we look on a globe, the island appears like a small spot in the Pacific Ocean, an error in the blue that fills the geographic map. And yet, on this small undecipherable piece of land stand the most mysterious statues of our planet, the Moai. Colossal stone heads, carved from the basaltic tuff of volcanic craters. Timeless gazes raising questions that today are still unanswered.

Who are the people portrayed in the faces of the Moai? The inhabitants of Rapa Nui in ancient times would have had to be capable, in some manner, of producing and transporting these monumental sculptures from one side of the island to the other. But how did they arrive at this enchanted, unreachable place? What watercraft did they use to cross thousands of miles of the Pacific Ocean?

Easter Island has a surface area of approximately 160 sq km (62 sq mi) and today numbers about 2000 inhabitants: it is the emerged portion of a volcanic massif, of which two great extinguished craters are clearly visible. The island was discovered on Easter day (hence its name) in 1722 by

c. AD 300 - Easter Island is populated by Polynesian peoples.

1722 - The Dutch navigator Jacob Roggeveen discovers the island on Easter day.

1877 - The local population is drastically reduced because of the slave trade and the spread of epidemics.

1888 - Easter Island is annexed by Chile.

1996 - The scientist Steven Fisher announces he has translated 22 tablets in the Rongo-Rongo language.

the Dutch admiral Jacob Roggeveen. According to his travel logs, the man who was then king of Rapa Nui told Roggeveen that he was the head of the last descendants of a vanished people: only those who had reached the island were saved; the rest of this ancient race no longer existed. Perhaps the sovereign referred to a civilization living on a large island that disappeared into the ocean, and toward which the gazes of the ancient Moai still face. The imposing statues still present on the island number nearly 600, although originally there must have been nearly twice as many. Despite being of different sizes (from just over 1 m to nearly 22 m, or 3.3 ft to 72.2 ft), they reproduce, obsessively, the same face. They all were fitted with eyes, nearly all of which have disappeared, and with special red head covers. The largest Moai produced – 21.5 m (70.5 ft), called "the Giant" – is still located in the Rano Raraku quarry, lying against the rocky wall from which it was sculpted. Among those standing, the tallest is called "Paro"; at 10 m (32.8 ft), it dominates the coast of Ahu Te Pito Kura. It has been calculated that at least 500 persons must have been required to stand it upright.

According to archaeologists, the first settlements on Easter Island date back to AD 300, people who succeeded in crossing the incredible oceanic expanses to arrive at the island, using ancient canoes. Scientists still debate whether they were Polynesian or South American, whether they came from the East or the West. Perhaps both hypotheses are true, because local legends tell of bloody feuds between two ethnic groups present on the ancient Rapa Nui, those of the "long ears" of Oriental origin, and those of the "short ears" of Occidental origin. A rivalry that degenerated to such a point that the "long ears" were massacred and their bodies dumped into a mass grave. The people of Rapa Nui encountered by Roggeveen believed they were the last survivors. But survivors of what?

There is another question at the center of the various scientific studies on Rapa Nui: how could the inhabitants of ancient times transport the great Moai from the quarries where they were produced all the way to the shores of the island? And yet they managed to hoist tonnes of stone without any knowledge of engineering, any draft animals, and perhaps not even the necessary utensils. According to a recent study performed on the island's fossil pollens, at the time of the construction of the Moai, the trees necessary for building systems of mechanical transport were not there. The wood on the island is said to have been exhausted around AD 800, before the Moai are thought to have been produced.Even more mysterious is the writing of the inhabitants of Rapa Nui during ancient times. In fact, archaeological finds known as the Rongo-Rongo tablets were discovered on the island. Unfortunately the majority of these were burned in bonfires ordered by the missionaries who arrived on the island. But it is surprising that none of the inhabitants knew how to read them because the complex symbolic writing on the tablets had been forgotten. And how is it possible that almost identical symbols were found at Mohenjo-daro, in the ancient Indus Valley, practically at the opposite end of the earth from Rapa Nui? The Rongo-Rongo language has not yet been deciphered, although in 1996, scientist Steven Fisher announced that he had successfully read 22 of the tablets. According to the scholar, the myth of creation was engraved upon them. The only thing certain is that this island, solitary and marvelous, at the center of an immense ocean, contains a puzzle that we have not yet been able to solve.

Index

Photo credits

Authors

Born in Rome in 1961, **Roberto Giacobbo** received his degree in economics and commerce. A freelance journalist and communications expert, he is docent of "New Media Theory and Technique" at the Faculty of Letters and Philosophy at the University of Ferrara. In 1984 he began his career in radio. He had his television debut in the early 1990s as program writer. Since 1997 he has been writing programs including *Misteri, Numero Zero, L'emozione della Vita* (produced in collaboration with BBC), *La Macchina del Tempo, Cominciamo Bene*, as well as directing Sportello Italia on the air for Rai International. He has also hosted the program *Stargate: Linea di confine*, which he has authored for Italian television channel LA7 since 1999. *Stargate* became Italy's first "television magazine" style program on the mysteries of archaeology and history, winning for two consecutive years the city of Trieste's international television prize in the research and culture category. He debuted on 20 May 2003 as author and host of the program *Voyager - ai confini della conoscenza*, joined, two years later, by the program *Ragazzi c'è Voyager!* The program has won many national awards in the fields of communications and television production. He has published several books, including *Il segreto di Leonardo (sulle tracce di Maria)* (2005); *Il ragionevole dubbio. Le risposte degli scienziati di fronte al mistero della vita oltre la vita* (2007); *Veniamo? La storia che ci manca* (2012) *Conosciamo davvero Gesù?* (2013), *La donna faraone* (2014). "Additionally" he has edited the series *Gli Atlanti di Voyager*.

Born in Rome in the mid-1970s, **Giulio Di Martino** received his degree in theoretical physics at the Sapienza University of Rome. After a period of research at New York University, he returned to Italy to write about science for major popular magazines. At the age of only 25 he began elaborating with RAI as a new media consultant. Since 2003 he has been writing for the program "Voyager – Ai confini della conoscenza," traveling all around the planet making documentaries on the most fascinating mysteries of history, science, and archaeology. One of these – "Isola di Pasqua" – even became a book. He also writes film and television dramas.